Harry Threlfall

The Time of my Life

To Olive Gold
With Best Wishes

Harry Threlfall

GoldStar Books

The Time of my Life

Copyright © 2010 Harry Threlfall

First published in Great Britain in 2010
by GoldStar Books, Bexleyheath, Kent
www.goldstarbooks.co.uk

British Library Cataloguing in Publication Data
A CIP catalogue record for this title is available from the British
Library.

ISBN: 1-904976-08-5

Printed by Orbital Print Ltd, Sittingbourne, Kent, England

Dedication

To my dear wife, Barbara,
the lodestar of my journey through life

Acknowledgements

When my son's father-in-law died fairly recently, Peter's wife, Vina, and her family were sad to realise that they knew very little about his early life. It was this that inspired me to write this autobiography for my own family.

My thanks go to Barbara for her patience and help whilst I was writing this book and to Mike Carver for his care in getting it ready for publication.

Chapter 1: When we were very young

It was a different world then in Scunthorpe where I spent the first twenty years of my life. It was one of the many agricultural villages of North Lincolnshire until the mid-nineteenth century when a local landowner, Rowland Winn, who was out with a shooting party near the village, tripped over a piece of rock. Some men would have cursed the rock and walked on but Mr Winn was of an enquiring mind; he picked up the rock, thought it looked interesting, and decided to have it investigated. The analysis showed that it was, in fact, iron ore.

Having not only an enquiring mind but also an eye for the main chance, Rowland Winn leased the land to the Dawes brothers who built a blast furnace and produced the first iron in 1864. As a result, Scunthorpe became a boom town; more iron and steel works were built and population growth soon absorbed the surrounding villages of Frodingham, Crosby, Brumby and Ashby.

In 1936 Scunthorpe became a borough and took for its motto "Refulget Labores Nostros Caelum" - *The Heavens Reflect Our Labours* – a reference to the lighting up of the whole sky when the molten slag from the blast furnaces was tipped on the slag heaps.

But enough of Scunthorpe for the moment – what of me? I was born in Scunthorpe in 1921 to Allan and Lily Threlfall and when I was very young, probably in 1924, I was adopted by my mother's aunt and uncle, Margaret and Ernest Brown. I never queried this arrangement, but just accepted it.

For the next three years of my life I lived in a fair-sized terrace house in Home Street in the centre of town together with the Browns ("Memmy and Unk" to me), my mother's cousin, Connie, my great-grandmother and great-grandfather, Ann and Henry Hollingsworth. This may seem a complicated arrangement but extended families living together were not unusual in those days. The house was big enough - it had obviously been built for Henry Hollingsworth as his initials and the date '1888' were engraved into the front façade - and everyone lived happily together.

A few words about family arrangements before the social reforms which were introduced after the Second World War. There was never any question of old people having to move into retirement homes - such places did not exist. It was customary for one of the children – usually a daughter – to stay in the family home and look after her parents when they became old. The only alternative for destitute old people with no relatives to support them was the workhouse - a dreadful institution in which men and women were separated and slept in dormitories. The regime was like that of a prison.

The nearest workhouse to Scunthorpe was at Brigg, eight miles away, and the expression 'going to Brigg' (said with fingers crossed!) meant suffering the ultimate degradation of being taken to the workhouse.

That was the Welfare State of the first half of the last century. There had been some relief for old people in 1908 when David Lloyd-George introduced the Old Age Pension which paid out five shillings a week (later increased to ten shillings a week) to people over seventy years old. Ten shillings was the equivalent of fifty pence in modern money but it represented almost a quarter of the average labourer's wage. One often heard the expression *going to the Post Office to collect my Lloyd George*!

Most houses in towns were built in terraces, in a continuous block that is. They usually had very small gardens. Number 21 Home Street, where we lived, had an alley between it and its neighbour with a front gate. On Friday and Saturday evenings men from some of the villages, especially Winterton about five miles away, would pay a few pence to park their bicycles there. Either there was no bus service or the parking fee was less than the bus fare! But to the residents it was an early example of private enterprise.

The kitchen was the hub of activity in the house. Cooking was done on a Yorkshire Range - a black monster which had to be 'blackleaded' regularly to keep it shining, rather like polishing black shoes. The range heated the kitchen and the oven, but there was no piped hot water supply and no bathroom. Baths were taken in a tin bath in the kitchen with hot water heated on the range – quite cosy, but not very glamorous!

Each of the three bedrooms had a jug and washbasin for morning and evening ablutions and, of course, a chamber pot. There was no lavatory in the house but an earth closet in an outhouse 'down the yard'. This raised problems if anyone was ill and I remember that when I had an attack of measles I was provided with a commode. If you don't know what that is look it up in the dictionary!

There was no electricity in the house and downstairs rooms were lit by gas mantles. I can still recall the distinctive small explosion as the gas jet ignited and the increasing light as the silk mantle heated up. Each bedroom was lit at bedtime by a portable oil lamp.

All this domestic detail may sound very primitive but my family were by no means poor and these conditions were fairly common among the working and lower middle classes.

The absence of any space for a garden in terraced housing was often compensated for by an allotment. My family had one a few hundred yards from the house and there was never any need to buy vegetables or flowers. Other food supplies came from the Co-op grocery shop, again, almost on the doorstep.

The Scunthorpe Co-operative Society was quite a force in the town with several grocery shops and, later on, a department store ... and even a cinema. Its main competitors in the town were branches of national grocery chains such as Maypole, Home and Colonial and Melias. But one of the attractions of the Co-op was its 'Dividend'. Every member of the society had a 'dividend number'. When you bought anything at the 'Stores' you quoted your number which was recorded with your purchase on the cash machine. I still remember our family numbers: 10726 and 11625!

Every year a dividend was declared – usually two shillings (i.e. 10 pence) in the pound (=10%) which was paid into your account. How the Co-op prices compared with those in private shops I have no idea but the Co-op and its 'divi' were certainly very popular. Supermarkets were unheard of. A customer in a grocery shop went to the counter and gave her order to the assistant who fetched most of the items from the shelves. Sugar was weighed out from a large container and put into 1lb or 2lb bags. Butter was taken from another bin, weighed, patted into shape and wrapped in greaseproof paper. The assistant wrote out a bill, the customer paid in cash, put the groceries in her shopping bags and left.

Home Street was only a stone's throw from Scunthorpe Church (St John's) which was the centre of the old town. There was a horse trough close to the church and although motorised delivery vans and lorries were increasing in number there were still horse-drawn vehicles on the streets including milk floats where you took your jug out to the milkman who filled it from the large milk churn carried on the float.

When great-grandfather Hollingsworth died in Scunthorpe Hospital in

1927 his body was brought back to the house, as was the custom, to lie in his coffin in the 'front room'. The funeral hearse was a magnificent glass-sided vehicle drawn by four black horses with black plumes.

The open marketplace was also quite close to Home Street but in the opposite direction from the Church. A market was held every Friday and Saturday. In the evening all the stalls were lit by naphtha flares – roaring naked flames fed from gas cylinders similar to the modern butane cylinders … but much more exciting! We had a personal interest in the market because Unk used to help out on a sweet stall owned by a Jewish family from Grimsby. Eventually, even our dog, Jack, grew tired of Cadbury's Dairy Milk Chocolate!

A few more aspects of life in Home Street: wireless, as it was then known, was in its infancy and there was only one broadcasting studio, which was in Savoy Hill, London. Its title was 2LO and it was owned by the British Broadcasting Company.

Earlier radio sets relied on what was referred to as a *cat's whisker* – a delicate wire which, by dint of much fiddling, was coaxed into contact with the correct spot on a crystal to detect the incoming signal, forming a sort of primitive diode or microchip. There was little, if any, amplification and certainly not enough power to operate a loudspeaker, so the solitary 'listener' to a 'crystal set' had to use headphones and request silence from everyone else in the room! We had a crystal set in Home Street, and it was considered miraculous to be able to hear in Scunthorpe the voice of someone speaking in a 'posh' accent nearly two hundred miles away!

A couple of a hundred yards away was a repertory theatre, the Empire, where I was sometimes taken by Memmy to see old favourites – mostly melodramas - such as *Uncle Tom's Cabin, Mrs Wiggs of the Cabbage Patch* and *East Lynn* ("Dead! Dead! And never called me Mother!")

I have no recollection of any cinemas or magic lantern shows at that time. The family had no interest in public houses nor, I'm afraid, churches. Evenings were generally spent gossiping round the fire in the kitchen or reading the newspaper, especially the local weekly *Scunthorpe and Frodingham Star.* Perhaps once a week Memmy, Unk and I would go round to a neighbour's house to play rummy or whist – both very good for improving an infant's arithmetic abilities, it has to be said!

My reading matter was limited to *Chick's Own* followed by *Tiger Tim's*

Weekly, all bought from Westoby's newsagents at the bottom of Home Street. When I was about five, I had a Hornby train set. I say 'train set', which sounds rather grand, but it consisted of one clockwork engine, a tender, two passenger coaches and a circular track. Not the best train set in the world but it meant a lot to me.

The only illness I recall suffering from at Home Street was measles which was quite serious in those days. There was never any question of being admitted to a hospital – I just stayed in bed and had daily visits from the old family physician, Dr 'Johnny' Walker. (I would love to have known how he travelled on his rounds but, unfortunately, I never shall!)

The only pain I still remember from those days occurred when I was taken across the road to see Fred Mee, the barber. The absence of electricity meant that the clippers Fred used on the neck and sideboards were operated by hand and, if Fred lost his concentration, they were liable to pull out the hairs by the roots.

Chapter 2: Now we are six

I started school in September 1926 just before I was five years old. The closest school to home was in Gurnell Street, about half a mile away, but the one in Crosby, about twice as distant, had a better reputation. Connie was by now a teacher and 'knew about these things' so it was Crosby that I went to. The infant school was mixed sexes but there were separate junior schools for girls and boys – the infants shared a playground with the junior girls.

I don't remember a great deal about the infant school ... except for one thing: the 'Fairy Letter e' at the end of a word magically changed the pronunciation of the vowel before it so that *fat* became *fate* and *bit* became *bite*, etcetera. Nowadays it's called phonetic spelling but to a four-year-old in 1926 the 'Fairy Letter e' was much more friendly!

In the first class in the infant school we used slates and crayons for writing but later on we graduated to pencil and paper and were allowed to wear something more civilised than the navy blue smocks we wore when we started.

In 1927, the family moved to a newly-built semi-detached house on Ferry Road in Crosby. Around the same time, I moved up into the junior boys' school where the Headmaster was Mr George Taylor. The only other teacher I remember was Hugh Gilgallon.

Most of the boys spent their last two years at the school in the top class under Mr Taylor and, sometimes, an assistant. There were about fifty boys in the class with pairs of boys sharing double desks that all faced the blackboard at the front. Teaching was very much 'chalk and talk' but we spent a great deal of time writing compositions and stories using steel-nibbed pens dipped into inkwells. We also practised copperplate handwriting.

Talking in class was a punishable offence. The register was called each morning before lessons and unexplained absence for a couple of days (which was rare) meant a visit to the home by the School Attendance Officer.

There was great emphasis on religious education – we could all recite the Ten Commandments from memory but I have to confess to some lack of understanding. I worked out that adultery must be something to do with grown-ups but I didn't know of any neighbours who had either an ox or an ass!

Arithmetic was much more difficult than it is nowadays - pocket calculators were not even dreamed of! Multiplication tables were recited in unison and never forgotten. Pre-decimal units made calculations extremely complicated what with inches, feet, yards, chains, rods, poles or perches, furlongs and miles for distances, ounces, pounds, stones, quarters, hundredweights and tons for weights and farthings, halfpennies, pennies, shillings and pounds for money. The sort of questions we got were "What is the area of a plot of land measuring 3 furlongs 27 yards by 5 furlongs 19 yards?" or "Find the total cost of 37 items priced at £1 13s 7d each.": Difficult to work out, but excellent for mental discipline!

The playground was very much as it is now except that the classroom which now fronts directly on to Sheffield Street was then just a part of the playground covered over for wet weather. On the opposite side of Frodingham Road from the War Memorial was a fish and chip shop. Diagonally across the crossroads was a Co-operative grocery store and near to it, on Frodingham Road, was a branch Post Office run by a rather grumpy old gentleman!

Facing the Co-op on Frodingham Road was Mr Dickinson's butcher shop. His son, John, was in my class and some of the other boys seemed to derive a macabre pleasure from hearing the squeals of pigs being slaughtered in the butcher's yard in the morning!

Behind Dickinson's, on Sheffield Street, was Mrs Patterson's sweet shop – a great attraction for those with a penny or two to spare. Behind the school, on Dale Street, was a rather decrepit building roofed with corrugated iron and always referred to as the "Micks and Pats". I always assumed it was a men's club with some Irish connection.

The school playground was very much as it is now except that the classroom which now fronts directly on to Sheffield Street was then just a part of the playground that was covered over for wet weather.

The most common game in the playground was 'Relievio' where one team took prisoners by 'tagging' (touching) them while the other team tried to penetrate the first team's defences and release them.

Individual entrepreneurs set up cigarette cards against the wall and invited punters to flick another card to knock one down and win it – a sort of playground coconut shy. Cigarette card collecting was very popular and 'swapping' was a flourishing activity.

In frosty weather (much more frequent than it is now) there were two or three big and well-used slides in the playground yet no-one ever seemed to get hurt. One beastly habit adopted by some boys in frosty weather was to approach another boy from behind and flick his cold ear with a finger: most painful, though the ear soon warmed up! I do not recall any use of bad language in the playground.

On Friday afternoons in the summer after school, several of us used to go to the Scunthorpe Baths for a swim. There were two separate pools - junior and adult - and entry for juniors was tuppence (two pence). Another good regular twopennyworth was one of the boys' comics – I never worked out why they were always referred to as comics because they mostly contained adventure stories. *Adventure, Wizard, Rover, Hotspur* and *Skipper* were the favourites; they were published on different days of the week and were freely swapped. *Magnet* and *Gem* were less popular - they were all about boys' public schools, like Greyfriars, and featured heroic boys like Bob Cherry and others - all destined to become leaders of men - as well as the ludicrously fat, greedy, underhanded Billy Bunter. I also used to read *The Children's Newspaper* edited by Arthur Mee who had previously published the ground-breaking ten volume *Children's Encyclopaedia* of which Connie had a complete set which was later passed on to me.

The whole school assembled in the playground for a service on Empire Day. And on Remembrance Day another service was held where a bugler played the Last Post before the two minutes silence was observed. The Great War had ended only ten years beforehand and we actually had our own war memorial in the playground.

On the last afternoon before Christmas, discipline was relaxed. Each boy was given an orange and brought a toy from home to share with the others. This would probably seem very dull to today's children but times were hard then and expectations were lower.

Although most of the boys at the school were local, some came from the more prosperous parts of the town, attracted by the achievements of the school and the reputation of its headmaster. George Taylor was a teacher of the old school: he believed in hard work and strict discipline enforced by use of the cane, neither of which was resented by the boys.

His nickname was Tadger and he instilled in all the boys fear and respect but, at the same time, loyalty and affection.

His standing was reinforced by wearing his academic dress (gown and mortar board) at all times in the school though I have since wondered if his academic qualification of 'Inter.B.A. (Lond.)' - as quoted on the War Memorial - really qualified him to do so! But no matter, it certainly strengthened his authority.

He was ambitious for his pupils and one of his main aims was to help as many of them as possible to gain a County Junior Scholarship which carried a free place at one of the County Grammar Schools in Scunthorpe, Brigg, Caistor or De Aston at Market Rasen. He recognised that this was their way out of their working class environment. And he was right. One boy I shared a desk with became a High Court Judge and many others went on to good universities of that era.

To help them pass these scholarship examinations, Mr Taylor held extra evening classes for several weeks beforehand and there were few absentees. Some might say that this was the same as the modern practice of helping children to get better grades in their SATs but not so: this was to help the boys improve their life prospects, not the school's grading.

*

The memorial in the school playground was erected soon after the end of the Great War in 1918 and was paid for from funds raised by George Taylor. It was dedicated to past pupils from the school who had given their lives during the course of the war. It also carries a memorial verse which I shall never forget, having seen it and read it every school day for five years:

The Last Despatch
Duty Done
Victory Won
Now for Peace
Every One
Carry On

George Taylor retired in 1934 - a year after I left the school - and went to live in Malvern. He was a fine man and a fine teacher but he would not fit into today's education system and that is this generation's loss.

*

Memmy, Unk, Great-Grandmother Hollingsworth and I had moved

Digging the new garden at
Crosby, aged seven

into 47 Ferry Road, Crosby in 1928. That part of Crosby, which was on the northwestern periphery of the Scunthorpe conurbation (if I dare use that rather flattering description), was being developed by small speculative builders who had bought tranches of land from the local landowner, Sir Berkeley Sheffield.

The buildings were mostly run-of-the-mill semi-detached three-bedroomed houses with a fairly large garden. For us, our new house was so much more convenient than the old house in Home Street.

We had electric lights in all the rooms, hot and cold running water and an upstairs bathroom with a flush lavatory. When we moved in, the land behind the garden was still pasture but soon diminished as more houses were built within the next year or two.

One attractive feature of Ferry Road was the public park that had been developed close to us on land donated by Sir Berkeley Sheffield. Not unexpectedly it was called "Sheffield Park" and it had plenty of grass areas for games, a children's playground with swings and seesaws, tennis courts, bowling greens, flower beds and a bandstand.

There was often a brass band concert on Sunday afternoons and Ferry Road was crowded with people in their Sunday best walking up to the park. It was quite a spectacle!

Memmy's sister, Ellen (Nen to me), and her husband, Fred Hornsby, had bought the other half of our semi-detached house and Connie and her sister, Freda, moved in with them. Freda worked as a secretary in the local Magistrates' Court while Connie had qualified as a teacher and was working at the Doncaster Road Senior Girls' School.

Fred Hornsby was a coal merchant, working on his own account, and he used to deliver bags of coal by horse and cart. The horse was stabled on an allotment off Normanby Road and Fred also kept a pig there which was fattened up for Christmas. I remember the annual processing of the porker and it did not appeal to me then any more than it would now, even though it provided plentiful sausages and some chitterlings! I am sure it would have given me a good grounding in anatomy but that was one part of the educational curriculum I was willing to forego.

*

Around this time (circa 1930) Connie had been courting George Robinson who had joined the Royal Air Force and was posted to India. I remember she used to stand at the gate waiting for the postman to deliver his weekly letter (complete with an Indian stamp which later found its way into my stamp album). I think George was stationed mostly in the northern part of what is now Pakistan and aircraft from his base used to patrol the northwest frontier. He was on a long-tem service contract – five or seven years - and later served in Iraq. Whether there was any leave during the contract I do not know, but it is doubtful.

Patience was not only a virtue but a necessity for engaged couples in that situation As the song has it:

> They say there's a troopship just leaving Bombay,
> Bound for Old Blighty shore,
> Heavily laden with time-expired men
> Bound for the land they adore.
> There's many an airman just finishing his time,
> There's many a twerp signing on.
> You'll get no promotion this side of the ocean,
> So cheer up my lads, Bless 'em all!

Connie and George were married in the early nineteen-thirties and had a few years' of married life together before George was called up as a reservist in 1939. Almost immediately, he was posted to an aircrew training station in Saskatchewan, Canada!

*

It was about half a mile from Ferry Road to Crosby School and I walked there and back twice daily. The morning session was from 9 am to 12 noon and the afternoon session ran from 1.30 to 4 pm. Walking to and from school was relatively safe in those days - there was not enough traffic for it to be dangerous. I was often with two friends who lived in the newly-built Sheffield Park Avenue which was adjacent to the park.

Spring, I remember, used to be the traditional season for playing marbles and we used to roll our marbles in the gutter all the way home when school had finished for the day. The common or garden clay marbles were called taws and the superior glass ones were known as glass alleys.

There was one house along the way whose name I shall never forget. Even in junior school I knew the owners should have given a little more thought to it. The poor house was called *Libido Nook*!

*

When pupils in junior schools reached eleven years of age they took the examination for a scholarship and, as I said before, at Crosby we got every help and encouragement from Mr Taylor.

The examination consisted of only two papers - one in arithmetic and one in English. Of my two friends, one - Gerald Pidd - gained a scholarship and went to Scunthorpe Grammar School; the other - Alec Ashmore - did not. But he still went to the same school because his parents paid for him.

I think the fee was £12 a term.

Chapter 3: Grammar School

Three things happened in 1933. Early in the year Great Grandmother Hollingsworth died; I think there may have been some sort of inheritance because later in the year we moved to a better, detached house in Sheffield Park Avenue, built to specification by a local builder and with a view over the park And I gained a County Scholarship to Scunthorpe Grammar School.

One of my most vivid recollections of this new phase in my life was of setting off on my new bicycle with my new schoolbag slung over my shoulder and having to walk through the park (cycling was strictly forbidden!). But I could then cycle the half mile to my new school.

Scunthorpe Grammar was quite a revelation and so different from my primary school. The other County Grammar Schools were fairly old foundations in old market towns but the Scunthorpe school had obviously been built in 1927 to satisfy a specific need in a rapidly growing industrial area. Nonetheless, although it did not cater for boarders, like the rest, it tried to follow the style of a public school.

The lowest form for eleven year olds was the Third Form followed by the Lower and Upper Fourth, Lower and Upper Fifth and Lower and Upper Sixth. The teachers were all graduates, wore academic gowns at all times in the school and taught only their own specialist subject - somewhat different from the multi-discipline teaching, albeit at a lower level, at Crosby School.

And there was homework every evening and different coloured books for each subject; to say nothing of mixed classes - girls in the classroom! – with only thirty pupils in each class. And a proper break half way through the morning with a hot drink and a bun in the dining room. We even had a timetable with a bell signifying the end of each period, rung by the redoubtable Miss MacGregor, the school secretary. She had an office next to the headmaster's. He was also called Taylor ('Sprutt' when he wasn't listening!).

The novelty of a timetable for lessons so impressed itself upon me that I can still recall the order of lessons for Monday and Tuesday: History,

English, French, Arithmetic, Geography, Biology, Games; French, Algebra, Geography, English, Arithmetic, Woodwork or Domestic Science (double).

All the classrooms were built around two quadrangles, with French windows along the side facing the quadrangle. The hall, also with French windows, was between the two quadrangles, with the library and the headmaster's study at one end and the gymnasium at the other.

A GYMNASIUM! A cut above Crosby School's playground! Yes, but can you spell it?

There was roughly the same number of men and women teachers, (Masters and Mistresses, as they were known to us) but it would have been improper for them to share a common room. So the women's common room was in one quad - usually referred to as the Girls' Quad – and the men were sited as far away as possible in the Boys' Quad.

The women were, of course, all 'Miss' because it was the regulation in those days that, when a woman in public service married, she had to resign her position. Masters were always addressed as 'Sir' and Mistresses as 'Miss' – the familiarity of Christian names was not even dreamed of except in the case of teachers addressing girls but boys were always called by their surname.

I don't think anyone knew where the Headmaster's nickname of 'Sprutt' came from but when his son came to teach maths at the school he was given the nickname of 'Young Sprutt'!

The chemistry teacher, Mr Hawkins, for some reason, was 'Faf' and was honoured with a scrap of doggerel verse:

Poor old Faf is dead and gone,
His voice you'll hear no more,
For what he thought was H_2O
Was H_2SO_4!

The only master who had a nickname acquired during my stay at the school was 'Spitter' Morris, the Geography teacher. During a camping trip with some of the boys he is said to have remarked about the countryside, 'I like it in the country - you can always have a good spit!' Which only goes to show you should be careful what you say in front of the boys!

Each form was split into three classes - A, B and C. On entry you were placed in Form 3A, 3B or 3C presumably determined by the academic standard you reached in the scholarship examination, or the entry examination (for paying pupils). A certain amount of promotion or demotion took place at the end of the first year and, on occasion, in later years. There was very little grouping by subject except that at the end of Year One there was a choice of Biology or Physics (this largely followed gender – guess which way) and Latin or German. At the end of Year Four there was a choice between Geography and Chemistry.

Examinations were held at the end of the Christmas and Summer terms – quite formal occasions with all desks moved into the hall and strict invigilation. Form positions, in each subject and overall, were allocated and were the subject of a certain amount of rivalry.

The first really serious external examination hurdle was the School Certificate, taken at the end of the Upper Fifth form year, the papers for which were set by one of half a dozen University Examination Boards – we used the Cambridge Board. The papers were in the following subjects: Biology, Chemistry, English Language, English Literature, French, Geography, German, History, Latin, Mathematics (consisting of Algebra, Arithmetic, Geometry) and Physics. In each paper you were awarded a Distinction, a Credit, a Pass or a Fail and you had to have at least five Passes or above to gain a School Certificate – it was all or nothing: a case of 'Live or Die' during an hour or so in the examination room. Five passes or more and you had a School Certificate; less than five and you had no School Certificate.

Most entrants did, in fact, gain a School Certificate except for some from the 'C' stream who may not have been entered anyway. There were probably about five hundred pupils in the school and after the School Certificate examinations about twenty stayed on into the Sixth Form, mainly the more academic types who were aiming for higher education such as Teacher Training College or University.

In the sixth form you generally took three main subjects; either chemistry, physics and mathematics or arts subjects such as English, a language or history, etcetera. I took English, French and Geography with Latin as a subsidiary subject.

Those who did not stay on in the sixth form usually found work locally and took up some form of training – nursing or secretarial for the girls and technical training at the steelworks for the boys. Remember that in those days the extra contribution which young school-leavers could make to the family budget was far preferable to the expense of sending them to college or university.

So, in 1938, I entered the sixth form and I think the next two years were the happiest of my school life. Less than half of my time was taken up with lessons (in classes of only half a dozen pupils and in subjects in which I was interested) and the other half was mostly spent in the library reading round my subject, writing essays or doing translations (Latin).

Sixth form at Scunthorpe Grammar School, 1938

My teachers were Miss McKay (French) and Messrs Mattam (English), Morris (Geography) and Culwick (Latin) – all very capable and pleasant teachers.

A shadow was cast over my first year in the sixth form by the growing cloud of international tension. The Munich Agreement was signed at the end of September 1938 and war with Germany was narrowly averted albeit at the cost of ceding to Germany the Sudetenland region of Czechoslovakia which contained the Czech military defences of its western border. In April, Germany cynically annexed the rest of Czechoslovakia and it became clear that conflict was almost inevitable.

War was declared at the end of the Summer holidays 1939 and all schools were closed for a couple of weeks until the authorities could see how civilian life was going to be affected. In fact, life did not change very much at first; food was rationed but not very severely; air raid shelters were built; gas masks were issued and were carried everywhere. But things became more serious the following Spring,

I became the editor of *The Scunthonian* (the school magazine) that year and included in the 1940 edition the following adaptation of Browning's poem:

HOME THOUGHTS, AT HOME
Oh! To be in England
Now that we're at war,
For whoever walks in England
Sees a thing he never saw,
That, the smallest child to the dignified man,
All carry a cardboard box or a can;
And shelters rise 'neath the orchard bough,
In England – now!

And after April, when all around us,
We see barricades surround us,
Defence volunteers watch all the skies,
Whence invaders may come in the modern fashion,
(Parashoot when you see the whites of their eyes!)
Air raid practice, and smaller butter ration.
We hope he will not damage with his Kultur
Our nice new air raid shelter.
And though the fields are gay with shining dew
Chaos will reign when sirens sound anew;
And, aeons hence, the wandering poet who sings
Will ask himself how we endured such things.

Whilst on the subject of the magazine, perhaps I could include a contrasting romantic verse which was included in the same issue:

BEAUTY
Roses when the moon is full, Oh! there
Beauty, dewy eyed and fragrant sleeps
Upon a silken couch; a whispering wind.
With sorrow sighs, a star in Heaven weeps

Beauty dies a thousand times a day
To rise in greater glory; roses fade
To spring again; thy blushing rose will mourn
And die with youth, a single bloom, fair maid.

This brings us to the question of how I first met Barbara. Our Geography teacher, Mr Morris, had the idea of interesting members of the fifth form in map reading (there was generally a question about map reading in the School Certificate Geography exam) and the making of simple maps. He co-opted members of the sixth form to help. So you could almost say Barbara and I first met over a prismatic compass and the problem of closing the traverse. Things never looked back after that!

*

I was never very good at games; indeed my only school achievement was to come fifth in the senior cross country race in my last year. But I feel it's worth mentioning a couple of details about football as it was played then. Football boots were not the flexible comfortable footwear they are now – they were made of stiff thick leather which was supposed to soften up when treated with a greasy substance called dubbin. But not mine! The result of all my efforts was a stiff thick leather which was now incredibly greasy! (The word 'dubbin', by the way, comes from the verb 'to dub' which is used to confer a knighthood. Interesting!)

I think the leather used to make football boots was also used to make the outer casing of footballs because if you were silly enough to head one you were instantly aware of the impact. I actually got much more pleasure from the impromptu games of football (and cricket) with half a dozen friends in Sheffield Park using rolled up coats for goalposts and having only three or four players a side.

*

For holidays, the family normally went to Blackpool for a week in the summer and I went with them until I was about sixteen. After that, I went with a friend.

Holidays with pay did not exist before 1938 and many men could not afford to lose a week's wages to take a holiday. In the north of England most families on holiday in the popular seaside towns like Blackpool stayed in boarding houses where the landlady provided a bedroom and a cooked breakfast but the protein for the midday meal (dinner) was bought by the boarder (meaning the wife) and was cooked by the landlady together with the potatoes and vegetables she provided. The cost of this service was included in the daily boarding charge which I think was about two shillings per person - about ten pence in decimal currency.

The return train fare from Scunthorpe to Blackpool for an adult was £1 0s 3d but remember the total weekly income of a well-paid working class family was less than five pounds.

Seaside landladies were an easy butt for the jokes of music hall comedians and they were usually satirised as parsimonious battleaxes. But Florrie Marsden, the landlady at 42 Adelaide Street where we stayed, did not fall into this category at all. She was quite kind and helpful. Facilities which all modern holidaymakers now take for granted, such as en suite shower rooms and lavatories, were never on the agenda. We were still in the age of the chamber pot under the bed and the loo down the landing, with a bath or shower scheduled for the first Saturday you were back at home.

Afternoons were spent on the beach, at the Pleasure Beach or in Stanley Park, weather permitting but there were also indoor entertainments in the Winter Gardens and the Tower and, in the evenings, plenty of theatres and music halls offered first class artistes, to say nothing of the Tower Circus.

One unique feature of the Lancashire cotton town was the institution of Wakes Weeks where the mills in each town closed for one week in the summer and all the workers debunked to Blackpool. Although Blackpool could be classed derogatively as a *popular resort* one was never conscious of any anti-social behaviour. In that respect, I think it has gone downhill and has also suffered from the relatively modern popularity of cheap package holidays abroad.

*

In the summer of 1940 I sat the examinations in Geography, English, French and Latin (Subsidiary) for the Cambridge Higher School Certificate and, along with most of the small number of my colleagues who did the same, was awarded a County Senior Scholarship on the basis of my results. This, like the Junior Scholarship, was sufficient to pay tuition fees at a university but not accommodation. Universities were not as overwhelmed with applications as they seem to be nowadays because no-one had decreed that half of all school leavers should go to university and be awarded a degree even if they had no academic inclination and did not require letters after their name to pursue the career they had in mind.

My colleagues and I had certainly given little thought to the question of a university before the examination, unlike pupils of public schools who often sat the entrance examination (popularly referred to as the *Little Go*) for a particular college at Oxford or Cambridge. This was done in the spring term of the year they wished to enter.

We all discussed the question with our teachers and the headmaster and made decisions and I decided to apply to St Catharine's College, Cambridge for two particular reasons: firstly, all headmasters tended to regard the sending of a pupil to Oxford or Cambridge as a feather in their personal cap (Sprutt was an incorrigible snob anyway!) and, secondly, because J.A.Steers, a Geography don at St Catharine's, had a good reputation in the academic world of geography. I was accepted and entered 'Cats' early in October 1940 at the beginning of Michaelmas term.

*

While we were concerned with examinations and universities, the German Army invaded and conquered Norway and Denmark in April, Holland, Belgium and France in May, and the British Army had been evacuated from Dunkirk, mostly without its arms and equipment. It was obvious the German Army would now try to invade Britain if it could gain air superiority over the English Channel by winning what came to be called the Battle of Britain.

The German Air Force (the Luftwaffe) started the action at the beginning of August by attacking several RAF aerodromes in an attempt to disable the force. The failure of this attempt was due in large part to (a) the British chain of radar stations along the south coast which enabled the RAF to detect the raiders before they reached the coast and (b) to the control rooms which used this information to direct the RAF fighters to their quarry.

Having failed to defeat the RAF, the Luftwaffe turned its attention to bombing London. The 7th September 1941 marked the beginning of The Blitz. The night bombing of London and other cities continued intermittently for the remainder of the war.

Chapter 4: Cambridge and the R.A.F

To fulfil the residential requirements of a degree course at Cambridge it was necessary to be resident in the university for a certain number of 'full terms' - a 'full term' being a period of, I think, sixty nights within the limits of a 'Long Term' which was something like seventy nights. So if you were a couple of days late coming up at the beginning of full term you could stay a couple of days longer at the end of term and still qualify.

If you wanted to spend any nights away from the university during full term, you had to get an 'exeat' from your tutor. (I mention this and similar requirements even though they may no longer apply because they are some of those quaint customs with origins lost in antiquity.)

Another requirement which may have fallen into disuse is that of being in your rooms by ten o'clock at night without another special permit. Unless you knew a way of climbing over the college wall you had to be booked in at the Porter's Lodge or suffer a fine of one penny! After eleven o'clock it was a fine of two pence and after midnight a summons to see your tutor the next day.

There were not enough rooms in college for all the undergraduates and some were placed in licensed lodgings that were reasonably close to the college. These were not licensed in the sense of selling drinks but were licensed by the college authorities as being suitable for college undergraduates. Above all there had to be a living room and a separate bedroom - as there were in college rooms. Both sets of rooms had to have access to bathrooms as well and one is reminded of the account of a visitor to one of the colleges some years earlier who commented to the Master about the lack of bathrooms.

'Bathrooms?' replied the Master. 'But the terms are only eight weeks long!'

Landladies of licensed lodgings had to do the same as the porter in the college lodge, i.e. lock the door at ten o'clock and book in any student coming in after that time.

Another little rule: ladies were allowed in college rooms or licensed lodgings but had to be out before a certain hour. I think it was eight o'clock.

When I first went up at the beginning of Michaelmas term 1940 first year undergraduates were put in licensed lodgings and my first lodgings were with a Mrs Rogers at the family's flower shop in Newnham Road. My most enduring memory of these rooms was the gorgeous smell of flowers which pervaded the whole house.

The lodgings were very conveniently situated for the college and the School of Geography and actually had a piano in the living room. All these attributes were no doubt reflected in the cost which was 18 guineas a term but I decided I must look for something cheaper for the next term.

There were so many things to sort out when I first arrived: I had to meet my tutor who turned out to be J.A.Steers himself; my ration book had to be apportioned between college (for dinner) and lodgings (for breakfast); I had to buy a St Catharine's College undergraduate gown (which had to be worn for lectures, supervisions, dinner in hall and at any time outdoors after dark.)

There were two or three lectures every morning in the School of Geography in Pembroke Street and supervisions once a week in the supervisor's study.

About four undergraduates attended a supervision for which they had prepared and written different essays, each of which was read out and commented on by the supervisor and the other students. I found this more valuable than the lectures, some of which, especially those of J.A.Steers, were very poorly delivered.

Being of an academic turn of mind rather than athletic, I was not really diverted from study by games societies and spent most of the rest of the week preparing my essay for supervision, and reading any books or papers recommended by lecturers. There was an excellent library in the School of Geography and the university library held more obscure items. There was also a library of sorts in college though it had not been maintained and was quite useless.

The Professor of Geography, by the way, was Frank Debenham who had been a member of Captain Scott's expedition to the South Pole. He was also Director of the Scott Polar Institute in Lensfield Road.

*

It was a college rule that all undergraduates had to have dinner in hall every evening except for the concession that you were allowed to sign off one evening each week - a concession I almost always took advantage of. Hall was a typical college hall – wood panelled with portraits of former Masters – with the dons sitting at High Table and the rest at about four tables running the length of the room.

I can still remember the beginning of the Grace: Oculi omnium aspiciunt et in te sperunt, Domine. Tu das iis … (I must try to find out the rest of it!) After dark, it was compulsory to wear one's gown, even when riding a bicycle to hall, which was rather awkward if it was raining.

University discipline was administered by a couple of dons, elected for a fixed period as Proctors, who patrolled the streets of Cambridge after dark accompanied by two sturdy college servants called Bulldogs. There is an amusing, though doubtless apocryphal, story of an undergraduate encountered in the street sans gown and accompanied by a young lady who happened to be known to the proctors. One of the bulldogs was immediately dispatched to speak to the undergraduate:

"Excuse me, sir, the Proctor would like to speak to you."

"Certainly!"

"Yes, sir!"

"Would you be kind enough to introduce me to the lady?" (The 'lady' was already known to the proctors as a local lady of the night.)

"Certainly, sir. This is my sister."

The Proctor, somewhat taken aback by this: "Are you sure, sir? Are you aware that your *sister* is one of the most notorious prostitutes in Cambridge?"

The undergraduate (in for a penny, in for a pound): "Yes, sir. Mummy's always going on at her about it but she won't change her ways!"

End of story!

*

I scarcely ever took lunch in hall although it was served every day. Usually, I went to Joe Lyons in Petty Cury and had a small meat pie and potatoes followed by a steamed pudding and custard - all for about one shilling and a penny. If I was feeling really extravagant, I lashed out another twopence for a cup of coffee – all this served at the table by a 'nippy' in the well-known Lyons uniform of black dress, white pinafore and white headdress.

On Sundays I was more adventurous and sought out a new restaurant each and every week.

*

At the end of term, early in December, I returned to Scunthorpe, as I had come – by train. My trunk was collected by the railway (LNER) lorry the day before I travelled and arrived the day after. The journey from Cambridge to Scunthorpe involved changes at Ely and March in the Fens, and then at Peterborough and Doncaster on the main line.

The Christmas vacation was about six weeks and it was good to be able to relax a little, see school friends again to exchange notes, and go out with Barbara. We had exchanged letters at least once a week while I had been away but face to face contact was so much more meaningful!

Before leaving Cambridge, I had arranged a change of lodgings to 35 Owlstone Road in Newnham. I forget the name of the landlady but, though it was further out of town, it was only 12 guineas a term! No lovely scent of flowers, though.

Barbara photographed when she worked at the Central Telephone Exchange, London, 1944

*

Back to Owlstone Road late in January for Lent term, I now had a little radio (called a wireless in those days) and I have clear memories of listening to news of the battles in the Western Desert around Tobruk which was taken by the allies in late January. There was also a very popular show - a sort of sitcom- called ITMA (It's That Man Again). It was a radio classic starring Tommy Handley and had such memorable catchphrases as 'Can I do you now, sir?' and 'I don't mind if I do' – perhaps not very amusing when repeated out of context seventy years later but they brought the house down in 1941.

All radio humour was so much simpler (and cleaner) then, possibly because the memory of Lord Reith still hung over the BBC. He had left in 1938 to become chairman of Imperial Airways, later renamed British Overseas Airways Corporation.

*

Since the previous October I had been a member of the university OTC (Officer Training Corps) and had spent every Thursday at their training centre on the university rugby ground on Grange Road. The first term was spent on basic infantry training followed by a specialist branch - I selected the Royal Artillery. Unfortunately (or was it?) I failed the final passing out exam and, with my age group soon coming up for national service, I realised some quick thinking was required.

On the other side of the coin, at about the same time, I sat the end of year Geography exam (officially the qualifying examination for the Geographical Tripos). I gained a first class pass which earned me a college prize (meaning a reduction in my college bill!)

This could be a good time to mention and enlarge on a small incident which occurred in the summer term. On a few occasions when the weather was warm I went swimming in the town outdoor swimming pool which was fed by the River Granta. A few days after one visit I realised I had developed a verruca on my foot - a rather painful subcutaneous wart. Such things were often caught in swimming pools and they warranted removal.

Now, before the National Health Service came into operation on 5th July 1948, a doctor ran his own practice as a private business, sometimes with a partner, sometimes starting up from scratch, sometimes buying a practice from a retiring doctor. Anyone needing medical attention went along to a doctor's surgery (generally by recommendation), had a consultation and, unless the condition needed hospital treatment, was given some medication made up by the doctor's own dispenser – a bottle of medicine, a jar of ointment or the like. Then, a little while later, the doctor sent him a bill – perhaps half a guinea for a visit and medicine.

I had never had any contact with doctors whilst I had been in Cambridge and decided the best thing to do might be to take myself to Addenbrooke's Hospital on Hills Road, which I did. It wasn't long before I was seen by a doctor who screened the rest of my toe and burned off the verruca with a sort of X-ray gun. On my way out, I was approached by a lady who introduced herself as the almoner and asked me if I could make a contribution, which I did.

That illustrates the organisation of medical services before the National Health Service. Hospitals were financed in a variety of ways – by charity, by endowments, by the local authority, but not by central government. I remember that the hospital in Scunthorpe was named 'The Scunthorpe and District War Memorial Hospital' because it had been founded by public subscription after the Great War in 1918. Presumably running costs were met by subscriptions from patients and contributions from local businesses and the like. There was also an annual hospital carnival preceded by a procession through the town of dozens of floats (and collection boxes!); it was very much a local community hospital.

I had really seen enough of the Army during my time at the OTC and eventually enlisted in the Royal Air Force as a radar mechanic. In August and September 1941 I was billeted in luxury blocks of flats in St John's Wood not far from Lord's Cricket Ground, and eating in Regent's Park Zoo! I spent most of my spare time exploring London either by bus or tube (I think it was a No. 82 bus into Piccadilly) and in general it was just a case of killing time.

Then I was posted down to Brighton for a few weeks, again just killing time. I remember that here I was billeted in a boarding house with about four other chaps, all sharing a largish bedroom with one 40W bulb: these things do tend to stick in the memory!

From there I was posted to RAF Scampton - a few miles north of Lincoln - to work in the wireless section. This was quite interesting and useful. Also, it was only an hour's bus ride from Scunthorpe! Scampton was the station from which the Lancasters flew on the Dam Busters' raid in May 1943 and in December 1941 there were only Wellington and Hampden bombers on the base.

After a few weeks I was posted up to Lancashire for a technical course at St Helens, the centre of Pilkington's glass industry, but first had to report in at an RAF base at Fazakerley (near Knotty Ash) in the suburbs of Liverpool.

The course was based at St Helens' Technical College and was intended to teach us all about electricity and wireless, both theoretical and practical. We learned about volts, amperes, ohms, watts, direct and alternating current, wavelength, frequency, etcetera, plus soldering and circuit assembly - all very interesting.

I was billeted with a very pleasant young couple with a small child; I forget their name but he was a Cambridge graduate and was a priest at one of the local churches. About half way through the course I contracted mumps - I think I caught it from the child – and spent a couple of weeks in St Helens Isolation Hospital then another week or two on sick leave. On my return I was, of course, in a different class but soon picked up the threads of the work.

In the RAF, St Helens, 1942
HRT is second from left on the back row

I was also in a different billet with a middle-aged couple - a Mr and Mrs Varlow. I think Mrs Varlow was missing something in her marriage but I could only surmise what it was. Mr V was a local builder and I was invited one evening to the local Freemasons' Ladies' Night, which was most entertaining. I also got to know Mrs V's niece, Sybil, who lived over the river in Wallasey. I subsequently made one or two voyages on the Mersey ferry to see her.

At the end of the course at St Helens I was posted to Cranwell to learn all about R.D.F. (Radio Direction Finding as it was then called - it soon acquired the name of Radar). Cranwell College was an elegant building near Cranwell village a few miles from Sleaford in South Lincolnshire. It was built as a residential college for cadet pilots entering the Royal Air Force, the RAF's equivalent of the Army's Sandhurst.

Since 1939, and with the great increase in numbers entering the RAF, the accommodation had been greatly expanded by building Nissen huts to serve as dormitories and larger equivalents for mess rooms, etcetera. Building on our basic wireless knowledge, we learned all about the maintenance of the two main types of radar station operated by the RAF: CH and CHL.

CH stations (abbreviation for Chain Home) were the originals, built in the later 1930s along the south and east coasts of England. They used very tall masts for their aerials to transmit a powerful radio blip and then to receive the reflected blip from the aircraft. If they had been lower, the blips would have been diverted upwards by reflection from the surface of the sea. The time lapse, measured electronically, between sending the signal and receiving it back indicated the distance of the aircraft from the transmitter. British aircraft carried a special device called IFF (Identification Friend or Foe) which sent back an amplified echo.

The CH stations were linked by landline to the plotting stations where members of the Women's Auxiliary Air Force (WAAFS) moved counters around a map table to show the positions of enemy aircraft (bandits) and British fighters to enable the flight controllers to direct the fighters to an interception point. This system had been one of the main factors in the successful outcome of the Battle of Britain ... from the British point of view!

The main drawbacks of the CH stations were that, firstly, despite using tall masts for their aerials, there was still a significant upward diversion of their 1.5 metre wavelength signals by the surface of the sea so that enemy aircraft could fly in at low level and not be detected; secondly, they did not detect the direction of the incoming aircraft.

These problems were solved when it was found possible to generate ultra-short wave radio signals (10 cms) using the newly-developed cavity magnetron. There was less reflection of short waves from the sea surface and a number of the shorter aerials could be mounted on a revolving gantry which could be linked to the receiver to show the direction from which the echoes were coming. The cavity magnetron, by the way, is nowadays the heart of the microwave cooker – another case of 'swords into ploughshares'!

At the end of the course in the autumn of 1942 we were all posted out to operational stations and I was posted to Kete which was a CHL station situated on St Anne's Head at the entrance to Milford Haven in

Pembrokeshire. It was at the top of steep cliffs formed of the local old red sandstone which were not only attractive but also helped to keep our radio 'blips' low over the sea. There were probably about thirty people on the station - all men - and included operators, mechanics, administrative staff, cooks, drivers, etc. We lived in a rather grand Victorian 'castle' just outside the village of Dale and worked on a shift system being shuttled the two or three miles between billet and operating station by truck. There were a few Canadian mechanics and I remember that three of them came from British Columbia, Saskatchewan and Windsor, Ontario which made for interesting conversation.

I actually celebrated my twenty-first birthday at Kete – with a cup of coffee made with granulated coffee, powdered milk and saccharine! There was very little aerial activity and I don't remember any unidentified aircraft on the screens. But one thing I do remember is the mild winter I passed there – no sign of snow, and blackberries on the hedges at Christmastime. We had 'Liberty Runs' once a week to either Milford Haven or Haverfordwest, neither of them a particularly exciting metropolis but a change from the isolation of Kete.

On leave, 1944

When I passed out of Cranwell I was recommended as a possible instructor and in the spring of 1943 I was posted there for just that purpose. I set about teaching the circuits and operation of the equipment I had first met a year ago. My fellow instructors were all very steady, intelligible chaps - several of them school masters - and life and routine was pleasant and orderly.

Jimmie Peacock, a friendly Scottish laddie, had been posted in from a radar station on the Isle of Tiree – you couldn't get much more isolated than that! Several times, I took him with me to Scunthorpe to Barbara's house and family. Scunthorpe was only a couple of bus rides away via Lincoln and I used to take advantage of the buses most weekends.

Later in the year I was sent on a short course at Malvern to learn all about a new piece of equipment. This was airborne and was fixed underneath a bomber aircraft to give the navigator a rudimentary map of the ground beneath enabling him to direct his bombs more-accurately onto his target. Only the recently-developed 10cm wavelength radio waves had made it possible to design a machine small enough to fit on an aircraft and the device was code-named H_2S because, as they said: *It stinks!*

A similar piece of equipment (called Mk 8) was designed to fit in the nose of a night-fighter aircraft to enable the pilot to see his target in the dark.

Returning to Cranwell after three weeks at Malvern, I had to pass on details about H_2S to incoming courses. I stayed there into 1944 with regular trips to Scunthorpe. In Spring, there was noticeably increased aerial activity on the airfields in the area, especially of gliders. Then, one morning when I was in the gymnasium, news came through that there had been landings on the coast of France. This was D-day!

A couple of days later, on a Saturday, Barbara and I met in Lincoln and went to a jeweller's shop to buy an engagement ring. Then we went to Scunthorpe to put it in place on the correct finger and show it off to the family.

We were officially engaged!

*

Later in 1944 I was posted to Yatesbury, another large RAF training centre. Yatesbury was situated to the north side of the A4 about five miles east of Calne on the western slopes of the Marlborough Downs. It was very pleasant countryside with rounded chalk hills, each with a crowning clump of trees – except for the one facing the main gate of the station which had a folly built on the crest.

Calne was the home of Harris, one of the largest makers of sausages and meat pies in the country. With the wind from the west, they made their olfactory presence very obvious and made regular guest appearances on the tables in the dining hall.

Bath was about fifteen miles to the west, and made for a very pleasant day out by bus. But my regular trips to Scunthorpe from Cranwell were very much missed!

One of the colleagues I remember clearly from Yatesbury was Ken Matheson who hailed from Liverpool. He was quite well educated but had incongruously worked as a debt or rent collector in some of the less salubrious districts of his home city. I remember his account of some local materfamilias in one run-down street tempting her offspring back to the family fold with the invitation in broad Scouse, "Cum 'ere an' ah'll knock yer bluddy 'ead in!"

I was still at Yatesbury on VE Day - Victory in Europe Day, 8th May 1945 - which was declared a public holiday. I hitch-hiked my way to London along the A4; to be at the heart of the celebrations was a 'never to be forgotten' experience. Yet I have no recollection of the return journey to Yatesbury!

Barbara's birthday fell in July and I remember being accompanied by a few friends to the Etam shop in Calne to buy a pair of cami-knickers as a present!

*

Soon after the end of hostilities, men's thoughts turned to demobilisation and a return to 'Civvy Street'. The government produced a demobilisation plan based generally on a *first in, first out* formula, but with exceptions where men with certain skills were needed to do civilian work. I fell into one of these categories in a way. During mobilisation, university students on science courses were exempt from call-up because they would probably be needed in some 'reserved occupation' after graduation, whilst arts students were called up in the general mobilisation. Now arts students (myself included) were to be allowed to take up their courses where they left off, if they wished to. I certainly wished to and the wheels were set in motion.

I was given a demobilisation book (identifying me as an ART student!) and had to get clearance from all the departments at Yatesbury. Then I was posted to the demobilisation centre at Cardington (near Bedford) which had been well known before the war as the base of the British air ships R100 and R101. There I was issued with everything the authorities deemed I might find necessary as a civilian. I was given a couple of weeks leave and pay and was finally cast out into the post-war world.

A general election took place about this time; there were no opinion polls to indicate the feeling in the country and it was a great surprise when Winston Churchill and the Conservatives were heavily defeated.

Chapter 5: Return to Cambridge and Marriage

Returning to Scunthorpe, I quickly got in touch with St Catharine's College and the Ministry of Education to finalise some of the details of my return to university. Lodgings were arranged at 42 Panton Street and I reported back to my college. And who do you think I reported to? None other than J.A.Steers.

I had no difficulty slipping back into the routine – lectures, supervisions, essays, hall dinners - the main difference seemed to be that there were several other returned 'veterans' like myself. It had been the practice to put freshers in licensed lodgings outside college and second and third year students in college rooms but things seemed to have changed during the war and it was now the freshers who lodged in college. As a result, I never had rooms in college.

*

Michaelmas term slipped by without incident, Christmas vacation as well. I do not have many memories of my second year except of buying an expensive jacket and flannel trousers from a branch of a Savile Row tailor in Cambridge!

During the summer term my thoughts (and Barbara's) turned to our wedding and my immediate responsibility was to find somewhere for us to live when we came up in October to spend a year in Cambridge. I ended my search at 17 Marlowe Road, the residence of Miss Connie Cowley, and it turned out to be a very fortunate choice. It was a terrace house in the quiet suburb of Newnham, probably dating back to the turn of the century, and with not many more amenities than 21 Home Street, Scunthorpe. There was no hot running water, cold water only in the back kitchen with jug and basin in the bedroom, an outside lavatory, a fireplace in our living room with our own coal supply outside the back door. But with Barbara as the lady of the house I knew it would be heaven on earth!

*

I sat my second year exam - Part 2 of the Geography Tripos - and got a II/1 which would count towards my Honours Degree. But my time in the services qualified me to take an Ordinary Degree then which I did in a ceremony at the Senate House. I was now entitled to wear a B.A. gown.

Back in Scunthorpe, preparations were under way for the wedding. Most couples were married in church in those days, combining a religious marriage with a civil marriage, but it was possible to be legally married with a just civil ceremony in a registry office.

We were married in St Lawrence's Church, Frodingham, where Barbara's mother and father had been married twenty-one years earlier on exactly the same date as us, 9th August, and even with the same priest, Canon Rust. Barbara's bridesmaid was her best friend, Barbara Leggott, and my best man was my brother, Cedric.

Weddings at that time followed a stricter code of etiquette than they

Our wedding at St Lawrence's Church, 1946

do now regarding who was responsible for what. The bride's parents, for instance, arranged the reception at the Berkeley Hotel; then there was the bridesmaid's dress, the flowers, the church fees, etc,etc. But it all went off like clockwork. At the end of the wedding ceremony the guests were taken down to the reception whilst the bride, groom, bridesmaid and best man were taken to the photographer's studio for the official photographs.

That was all the photography that took place then we were taken to rejoin the guests.

At the end of the reception the four principals slipped off to get changed into going-away clothes and then were re-united with the guests at the railway station to be 'seen off' on their honeymoon. There were never any arrangements in those days for a late night dance for all the young people.

An amusing episode (of which we never learned the outcome) was that at the station was another wedding party seeing off a girl who had just been married by her father, the vicar of Appleby, a village a few miles away. It later transpired that the bridegroom was already married so the vicar had just solemnized his own daughter's bigamous marriage!

Apparently the actual circumstances became known after the 'happy couple' had departed which resulted in a frantic search for the couple in order to save the bride's honour.

We would dearly have loved to learn the outcome but it was not to be!

We spent our first night of marriage at the Paddington Hotel near Paddington Station ready for an easy departure in the morning by train to Cornwall.

During the last part of the journey in Devon the track ran alongside the mahogany coloured old red sandstone cliffs on the right and the seashore on the left – most attractive.

Author on honeymoon in Penzance, 1946

We stayed in a guest house in Penzance and encountered our first embarrassment: Barbara's identity card and ration book were still in her maiden name! Nowadays this would not cause the slightest blush but at that time an unmarried couple would often sign in as a 'Mr and Mrs Smith' who had unfortunately mislaid their ration cards.

I do not remember a great deal about Penzance except that, although this was early August, there was none of the overcrowding you might expect at a popular seaside resort. I think it was probably too soon after the war for people to have settled down to routine seaside holidays.

There were some lovely fishing villages within easy reach but having no car we found the local bus service very useful. We visited Newlyn, Marazion, St Michael's Mount, Land's End, etc., and for those interested in heights on Ordnance Survey maps I append this quotation from 'Plane Surveying' by David Clark:

> 'To define the relative altitude of a series of points, it is sufficient to ascertain their elevations above any one datum surface ... The standard datum of Great Britain is that of the Ordnance Survey. This was originally the assumed mean sea level of the sea at Liverpool. With the object of establishing mean sea level with greater precision, hourly observations were made at Newlyn, in Cornwall, during the six years 1915-1921. Mean sea level at Newlyn is the new Ordnance datum ...'

After the honeymoon we stayed in Scunthorpe until early in October when it was time to go to Cambridge for the beginning of 1946 Michaelmas full term. Barbara soon established herself as the housewife at 17 Marlowe Road and formed good relations with Connie Cowley.

She also met two young ladies locally who offered to take her along to join the Cambridge Bach Choir. She was auditioned by David Wilcocks who was then the Organ Scholar at King's College and later became famous as conductor of the Three Choirs Festival and the King's College Choir.

We soon became accustomed to coping with rationing – a shilling's worth of meat a week and a few ounces of sugar and butter. We even tried snoek and whale meat (off the ration) but soon abandoned them though we did give the thumbs up to peanut butter (likewise).

Our neighbours on one side were the Misses Smith. They were very sweet but could not pronounce our name so we became 'Mrs Barbara' and 'Mrs Barbara's Husband'. Our milk was delivered by milk float and ladled into our jug from the churn. We always knew when the milkman had arrived from the loud bellow which came from the street: 'Merrrrllk!!!' If you didn't respond, you got no milk!

We made two good friends soon after we arrived: Jim Haslam and Cliff Smith were both reading Geography in the same year as myself; they both came from Blackpool Grammar School and had rooms in college. We quickly organised a pontoon school, meeting every Friday evening, alternating between one of their rooms and Marlowe Road. We also had a joint entry on the football pools and actually had a modest win one week. Happy Days!

*

The 1946-47 winter was terrible. Heavy snowfalls disrupted road and rail traffic and caused serious power cuts - both industrial and domestic. It was a disastrous start for the new Labour government under Clement Attlee.

The wintry weather continued and we were always amused when Connie Cowley went out of the front door every ten minutes to sweep up the half inch of snow that had fallen since she last went out!

After the frost and the snow came the thaw: the upper reaches of the Fenland rivers melted before the lower

The Backs, Cambridge

courses, burst their banks and flooded the low-lying countryside including parts of Cambridge. However, winter eventually turned to spring with glorious daffodils along the Backs and summer finally arrived with punts out on the river.

In May I took Part 2 of the Geography Tripos and achieved another II/1. Then we went to the Cats' May Ball. Almost every college organised its own May Ball during May Week, which was actually the first week in June. These were high class affairs – black tie, posh frock, two or three bands with the event lasting late into the night. At the end of the ball it was traditional to punt up river to Grantchester ... which we did (or rather we got half way), and then we went home for a rest. A wonderful end to the year!

Then came the thought, 'What do we do now?'

Graduation, 1946

England was not a very comfortable place at the end of the war. Rationing was still in force, there was a shortage of housing, everything was run down and in a bad state of repair. One's mind turned to somewhere overseas and I had the ideal qualifications for a job abroad.

There were not a lot of openings for surveyors in England but overseas, especially in the Colonies, there was plenty of opportunity. So I wrote to the Colonial Office who invited me to attend an interview in London. Soon afterwards I received a letter offering me a post as a surveyor in Nigeria. With memories of the description of West Africa as 'The White Man's Grave' I was less than enthusiastic about this and sent a polite reply to say so.

While reconsidering my future, I approached the Anglo-Iranian Oil Company and was offered a post of surveyor in Iran. The main drawback to accepting was that I was not allowed to take my wife for the first three years. Rashly, I accepted the offer.

Rashly? Yes ... rather: Barbara announced she was pregnant!

Meanwhile, I had received a tropical clothing allowance and clothes coupons which I had spent.

Very soon afterwards, another letter arrived from the Colonial Office: 'Would I be interested in taking a post in Tanganyika?'

Yes, indeed I would, but what about Iran?

I wrote a very apologetic letter to the Anglo-Iranian Oil Company who graciously accepted my resignation and even allowed me to keep the cash and coupons for my tropical kit! What gentlemen!

With our first baby, Susan, in 1946

I wrote to accept the post in Tanganyika and eagerly awaited developments. First, I learned I had to go on a Colonial Office Survey Course which was held near Longleat in Wiltshire. I went down first, found some digs nearby, and was then joined by the pregnant Barbara.

There were only half a dozen or so people on the course which offered a lot of practical experience to supplement the more theoretical nature of Cambridge courses. I particularly remember doing a night star observation in the garden of our digs with Barbara and our unborn child booking figures for me while I observed a star in the theodolite on a very frosty night. Greater love hath no woman....!

*

We left Longleat at Easter shortly after I had heard Blackpool winning the FA Cup on the radio.

Susan was born on the 16th May at Scunthorpe Maternity Home in Brumby Wood Lane. We did little else for the next couple of months except prepare for our move, including buying a second hand sewing machine (which proved to be an excellent investment) and a stout wooden crate for heavier items.

Early in July we all (Susan included) went to Leeds to have yellow fever inoculations.

Susan was also baptised by Canon Rust at St Lawrence's Church.

General view of Enborne Kennels

Rosie

Yoll with Aphrodite

Yoll again

Nancy, Yoll, Jinks, Doodle, Inge and Jessica - April 1992

Rood Hill House in Winter

Family group at Rood Hill House

Barbara and Harry on holiday in Montreux, 2006

These days crosswords require
more concentration

Barbara's birthday present,
1990

Chapter 6: Tanganyika

Dior's 'New Look' was just coming into fashion at this time and Barbara invested in a couple of dresses in the new style. On 5th August we set off for London's King's Cross and then on to Charing Cross after which we boarded the Llangibby Castle at Tilbury Docks.

We were on our way!

On board the Llangibby Castle, 1948

Never having been out of the country before, we found the voyage both interesting and exciting; firstly travelling along the English south coast in darkness with all the coastal lights passing in the distance; crossing the Bay of Biscay while we slept then passing Gibraltar before arriving at our first port of call, Marseille, where we went ashore and had a meal in the Old Port.

Then we travelled on to Genoa where we found time to have a good look around. We were surprised to find the shops were much better stocked than those back in England, particularly with good quality fabrics. We took Susan ashore in her Silver Cross high pram which was a great novelty to the Italian passers-by. They virtually mobbed the 'bambina' in admiration.

We were extremely short of Italian Lira but I found a way to increase our stock. In the city I came across a sort of currency market where cigarettes were treated as cash. I bought boxes of cigarettes in the shop on board our ship and took them ashore, soon getting to know a lady who dealt in such things. I handed over a box of cigarettes and she plunged her hand down her bosom, producing the necessary paper money for me in exchange. I'm not sure where she put the cigarettes!

After Genoa we sailed south and passed through the Straits of Messina between Italy and Sicily, only a couple of miles wide, then on to Port Said where the ship was invaded by traders dealing in local leatherware – handbags, pouffes, etc.

The Suez Canal, a narrow channel with desert on either side, joins a couple of large lakes between the Mediterranean Sea and the Gulf of Suez in the Red Sea. I should mention here that the Llangibby Castle was, like many passenger liners, also a freight carrier, and some days were spent in ports loading and offloading cargo, as was the case at our next port of call.

Mombasa, the chief port of Kenya, is often called Kilindini which means in Kiswahili *At the Deep Water* because the port in the old town is shallow, suitable only for native fishing boats and dhows (the lateen-rigged large wooden boats which trade across the Indian Ocean with Arabia, depending on the monsoon winds). Deep water berths had to be built to accommodate large ocean-going ships as Kenya's trade increased.

Leaving Mombasa we bypassed Tanga, the second port of Tanganyika and came to Dar es Salaam, our port of disembarkation.

We had arrived!

*

Dar es Salaam harbour is most picturesque. It is semi-circular in shape with a diameter of almost a mile and has a very narrow entrance channel from the Indian Ocean. The name in Arabic means *Haven of Peace.*

The city is built along the semi-circular northern side of the harbour overlooking the water. There were no deep water berths for ships in 1948 so we, and our baggage, had to be ferried to the shore by tender.

After going through Customs we were met by Willie Errit, one of the computing section of the Survey Department. He took us to our temporary accommodation at Mgulani Camp which consisted of a number of 'bandas' plus dining hall and recreation room ... originally built to house members of the Groundnuts Scheme on their way up country.

Our banda at Mgulani

A few words of explanation are called for here, I think! A 'banda' is a thatched one- or two-roomed building. The Groundnuts Scheme was dreamt up by the British government and involved the cultivation of tracts of land in central and southern Tanganyika to grow peanuts to reduce the world shortage of vegetable fats. The Tanganyika government *borrowed* a few of these bandas in preference to hotel rooms to accommodate people, like ourselves, for whom a house was not yet available.

The Groundnut Scheme, incidentally, proved to be an expensive failure.

So there we were: a young couple with a four-month-old baby in a two-roomed banda several miles out of town with no transport of our own!

It wasn't too bad for me: I was picked up by the survey lorry every morning and was taken in to the Survey Department where I worked all day before being taken back in the afternoon. But Barbara was stuck in the camp.

There was a 'liberty bus' into town every day but it was scarcely practical for taking a young baby in a high pram who needed feeding regularly.

We set our hearts on acquiring three items (not being too greedy!) by Christmas: a house, a car, and a fridge. I pestered Maudie Watts, the Woman Admin Officer, who was responsible for house allocation. She eventually came up with T17, bless her heart! It was in Oyster Bay a residential suburb to the north of Dar where the houses were occupied mostly by government officers like ourselves. The 'T' signified that it was intended to be temporary but we know it was still there - and occupied - in 1992!

The thatched building had a living room, two bedrooms, a bathroom and an external kitchen with a wood-burning stove. Complete with outside servants' quarters it all stood in a plot of about one acre. Houses and basic furniture were provided by the Government for a modest rent but the chairs needed covers and the windows needed curtains, which is where our sewing machine came in useful.

Having acquired the house well before Christmas, our next urgent requirement was a car as there was no bus service except to the African quarter.

British cars were available but while they might have been fine on the tarmac roads in town they were by no means sturdy enough for the country roads which were just bare earth. They became so rutted in the dry season they could shake a car to pieces yet they turned into slimy mud when it rained. American cars were much more suitable for the East African roads but they were only imported in limited numbers and it was virtually impossible to get a permit to buy one.

Since I was expecting to carry a number of African staff members, the best alternative appeared to be a box body built on to a Bedford 30 cwt truck chassis ... and this is what we did. The chassis came from Motor Mart & Exchange, the local Bedford and Chevrolet dealer, and the box body was built to our requirements by a woodworking firm, Keshaji Ramji. The resulting beauty became a member of the family and was familiarly known as *Emma*.

Emma

Emma certainly had a few idiosyncrasies: she did not have synchromesh gears which meant that one had to double declutch when changing gear, i.e. slide gear change into neutral, slow down or speed up the engine, then carefully engage the new gear ... not too difficult except that it did require longer legs than Barbara possessed. Her gear changes involved a certain amount of bottom shuffling on the seat!

And the non-electric windscreen wiper was powered by the suction in the engine inlet manifold which meant that if you were using the wiper in pouring rain and came to a slope which needed more pressure on the accelerator the wiper would virtually grind to a halt.

Also, we found that when we drove up country the atmospheric pressure decreased as the altitude increased. This affected the air/petrol ratio in the carburettor and caused the engine to 'pink' (emit a regular metallic noise). The solution was to retard the ignition by rotating the carburettor.

She also needed quite a bit of routine maintenance. Unlike modern cars, all the joints in the suspension and steering had grease nipples which had to be lubricated regularly using a grease gun. And she responded well to regular adjustment of her tappets, bless her! These experiences may sound off-putting for those used to computer-controlled engine management systems but we were nonetheless very fond of our first 'car'.

*

But back to the domesticity of the house. Circumstances and convention demanded that you employed a number of servants.

The wood-burning stove was in an outside kitchen but, with the ambient temperature often in the eighties or nineties, the temperature inside the kitchen was quite intolerable for a European woman. So you had to have an African cook (mpishi) who would not, for instance, prepare vegetables or wash dishes. That meant you also had to have a cook's assistant (mpishi boy). Nor was it part of the cook's duties to bring the food to the table – that was the houseboy's job who, luckily, would combine that with generally keeping the house clean and tidy. But the houseboy did not wash clothes – that was the work of a 'dhobi'!

Our staff at T17, Oyster Bay

Taking the demarcation of duties a step further, the dhobi did not wash children's clothes – that was for the ayah who looked after the child.

And, finally, someone had to keep the garden tidy, even if that meant no more than cutting the grass with a metal slasher: that was the garden (shamba) boy.

So there we have the full complement - mpishi, mpishi boy, houseboy, dhobi, ayah and shamba boy.

The basic currency in Tanganyika was the East Africa Shilling which was on par with the English Shilling. But pounds were never used in East Africa. So the monthly wages of those six servants listed above were (in the same order) - as far as I can remember - S60, S25, S50, S40, S50 and S25, making a total of S250 (or £12.50).

My annual salary - remember I was starting at the bottom of the scale - was about £600, or £50 a month, so the servants who were a virtual necessity took about a quarter of my salary. Consequently, money was a little tight in those early days and life at home for Barbara was rather boring with no real domestic duties to handle herself. So she soon found a little job which was right up her street.

The Secretariat was the headquarters of Government, rather like Whitehall in England but all in one building, and they needed a telephone operator. Since that had been Barbara's job in England she was soon appointed and found working at the heart of government was most interesting.

The Secretariat building was on the waterfront facing the harbour. It was almost next door to my office in the Department of Lands and Surveys - both ideal situations and very convenient for transport.

At that time, the only air link between England and East Africa was the seaplane service which stopped overnight in Malta, Cairo, Khartoum, Entebbe and Dar es Salaam, with hotel accommodation for transit passengers. I mention this because it landed on the harbour right in front of Barbara's switchboard at eleven o'clock every Saturday which was a most attractive beginning to the weekend!

*

Most of the survey work in Tanganyika was cadastral, i.e. marking out the ground and making plans of property boundaries. In England the boundaries of properties are 'general', i.e. not clearly defined, but in Tanganyika (and most other countries) they are clearly marked on the ground by concrete beacons. Once marked and surveyed they can easily be replaced in their correct position should they be removed or lost thereby avoiding the disputes which can arise with general boundaries.

In Tanganyika all land belonged to the government - except some properties, mostly farms, where the previous German government had granted freehold status - and was transferred to individuals only on leases for 33 or 99 years. This lease could not be entered in the Land Registry until it had been officially surveyed and a plan made. And because a mortgage could not be obtained without the security of a registered property there was considerable pressure to survey individual properties.

Since most of my work was around the town and I was using Emma to transport my equipment and survey gang, it was not difficult to pick Barbara up and go home for lunch, collecting her again at four o'clock. Office hours were 7.30 to noon and 1.30 to 4 pm from Monday to Friday, and 7.30 till noon on Saturdays.

Sometimes when I was working on the outskirts of the town I used to buy fruit from the locals - mangos, pineapples or coconuts - and put them in the back of Emma. One day when I had done this I met Barbara at four and we decided to do a little shopping on the way home. Emma was just rolling gently to rest in front of Seifi Stores and I pressed harder on the brake pedal to stop. But she continued to roll … right into the car parked in front which was pushed backwards into the car behind it! I realised (just too late) what had happened and summed it up with my impassioned comment, "That bloody coconut!" The offending offspring of a coconut palm had rolled forward and lodged itself underneath the brake pedal!

I cannot remember what the outcome was but there just happened to be an English police officer, also doing his shopping nearby, who smoothed things over for me. I don't think too much damage was done - certainly not to the sturdy Emma.

On the subject of fruit, an African would often come round to the house on a bicycle with a large basket on the rear containing all kinds of local fruit for sale - all fresh and cheap. And another unusual home service was regularly performed by an Indian barber who would come round on his bicycle, carrying a leather bag (just like a district nurse), and proceed to give me a haircut sitting on my own chair in my own garden! There were several of these guys doing the rounds and they were all dressed identically with round black hats. I think they must all have belonged to the same caste.

*

There were three main ethnic groups in Dar es Salaam: the Bantu -

black Africans who lived mostly in high-density housing in the west of the city; Asians, both Hindu and Muslim, living mostly in the centre (the commercial quarter) and Europeans mostly living in the suburb of Oyster Bay in the north.

The three groups coexisted happily because they complemented each other; there was no racial tension because, to use a well-worn cliché, everyone knew his place. The Europeans (almost entirely British) occupied government posts from the Governor down to the District Officer, as well as professional posts in the technical departments and senior posts in the European commercial concerns.

The Asians were the middle tier in commercial and government offices – clerks and also those in charge of Asian commercial firms, both large and small, down to the smallest 'duka' or corner shop. Most of the shops in the town were Asian owned and run.

The Africans did most of the lower grade work as labourers, messengers and domestic servants. There was no official colour bar but there was very little mixing amongst the ethnic groups.

*

During the hot season - between October and March - the warm sea was very tempting for bathing. At Oyster Bay, a coral reef a few hundred yards offshore kept out both dangerous fish and large ocean waves. And coconut palms on the landward side of the beach provided excellent shelter for picnics.

There was also a good beach at Mjimwema, south of the harbour, but to reach it you had to take the ferry which operated across the narrow entrance to the harbour. We went there several times with parties of friends and Susan soon became attached to the water.

*

We made a number of good friends in Dar. Mary and Gordon Gray were our neighbours to the rear of T17 and we first met them while we were putting out a fire in the grassy area between our homes.

They had a friend - always known as Bunty - who also worked in government. Bunty never let you forget that before she came out she had been employed as a secretary with Lazard Brothers - a very up-market banking firm in the City - and this governmental job was rather beneath her! I shall never forget the occasion when we gave her a lift in Emma - never the equivalent of the Bentley that might have been more to her taste! As we passed over a rather large hole in the road, the hammock seat in the rear came out of its sockets and deposited Bunty in an undignified heap on the floor!

She didn't accept any more lifts in Emma!

Emma also came in useful during rehearsals for one of the pantomimes. For some reason the piano was needed elsewhere and we agreed to transport it in Emma. We aroused some curious looks as we drove through the streets of Dar with a group in the back of Emma singing and playing the piano on the move!

The cast of Dick Whittington, 1949

We also belonged to the Dramatic Society in Dar. I cannot recall any of the plays we staged but I do remember two splendid pantomimes - *Aladdin* for Christmas 1949 and *Dick Whittington* for Christmas 1950 - in both of which Barbara had a singing part.

*

John Stoddard, another good friend, came out to Tanganyika a few months after us. He arrived with his new wife, Avis, soon after they had married in Singapore. He was also a surveyor.

In August 1950 I was posted to Iringa in the Southern Highlands to take over from A.F.M.(Alec) Smith who was departing on leave. We drove up in Emma and it was on this journey that I had to stop and change the timing on Emma's engine to cut out the pinking.

Iringa is situated at about 5000 feet above sea level and we certainly noticed the difference in temperature as soon as we arrived. Having wood fires in the sitting room was quite a novelty after the heat of Dar es Salaam.

There was no electricity in Iringa and we were glad we had the foresight to buy an absorption refrigerator which would operate on paraffin if necessary. In a normal electric compression refrigerator the refrigerant fluid is circulated by an electric motor but in an absorption refrigerator the circulation of the refrigerant is driven by heat supplied by either an electric heating element (as ours was in Dar es Salaam) or by a paraffin flame, as in Iringa. Not many people nowadays will have heard of a paraffin-driven refrigerator but ours was a Godsend in Iringa … so long as we remembered to keep the paraffin tank filled up! When I was working outside the town, I always tried to bring back some dried wood for the wood-burning cooking stove and sitting room fire.

*

Another difference: fuel supplies.

Petrol was not delivered to a petrol station by tanker or pumped into the car's petrol tank by the gallon as is done nowadays. Instead, it was delivered by lorry to the local Indian 'duka' in four-gallon tin cans measuring approximately eight inches square by a foot high. These containers, called debis, were then opened as required and were poured straight into the petrol tank. Unfortunately, debis tended to suffer from the banging about they had endured on the terrible roads from the depot and frequently leaked. The custom then was to weigh each debe before opening it to check that it still contained its full four gallons of petrol.

*

We made two good friends in Iringa – Maurice and Muffy Leach. They had a six-year-old son, John. As there was no school in Iringa Muffy received written lessons from the Government Education Department in Dar es Salaam which she was supposed to use to teach John. She found this very difficult because John just would not pay any attention to his mother and she was soon in despair. So Barbara and Muffy came to an arrangement: Barbara would take on the role of teacher whilst Muffy looked after Susan. This worked very well with John paying more attention to a 'teacher' than he ever did to his mother. Everyone was

51

happy!

Iringa's cool climate attracted European settlers and farmers and it was the centre of flourishing agricultural production; maize, vegetables, tea, pyrethrum (a constituent of insecticidal sprays), and tobacco all grew in abundance.

A number of the farmers were Greek and we were actually invited to a Greek wedding while we were there.

*

We were due to go on leave about April 1951 and we had discovered there were some more robust British cars coming on to the market so we decided to sell Emma and buy a Standard Vanguard Estate Car which seemed to have quite a good reputation.

It transpired the first Vanguards were not well designed for local conditions because the doors closed up to the floor of the car and let in clouds of dust from the dirt roads. But they were soon modified so that the closed door fitted over the floor and kept out the dust.

So Emma was sold to a local farmer. Timmy, the Smith's little dog whom we had looked after during their leave, was restored to them and I handed over the survey department to my successor whose name I cannot now remember. Off we went to Dar es Salaam to board the SS Mulbera headed for England.

The Mulbera was a British India line ship, much smaller and older than the Llangibby Castle. I think she dated from the 1920s and most of the crew were Lascars (from India or south east Asia). By contrast, on the Llangibby Castle they had all been British. With our Mulbera crew there was a different curry on the menu every day.

The Mulbera was one of a family of sister ships – the other three were the Matiana, the Madura and the Modasa. I believe the Prince of Wales - later King Edward VIII - had travelled on one of them for a visit to Kenya in the 1930s.

We had a leisurely voyage back to England and were met at Tilbury by several members of the family, all anxious to see three-year-old Susan.

Soon after our arrival we picked up the new Standard Vanguard and drove up to Scunthorpe. We had made no arrangements to stay anywhere definite while we were on leave and spent most of the time either with Barbara's parents at 59 West Common Lane or with Memmy and Unk at Sheffield Park Avenue. This was not the best of arrangements, and we soon realised we should have been more independent.

At the end of this leave, in October 1951 or thereabouts, I learned I was needed back in Tanganyika to replace someone going on leave from Moshi. So I had to return by air and I handed the Vanguard to a shipping agent in London to follow on with the again pregnant Barbara and Susan in (I think) the Madura.

I travelled in a Hermes aircraft which I had never previously heard of ... nor have I heard of one since! There was some trouble around this time over the Iranian oilfields - which had just been nationalised - and there was a possibility that the Suez Canal might be closed. In that case, the Madura would have to travel south around South Africa and the latest addition to our family could conceivably be born aboard ship. This was of more than a little concern to Barbara because all her nappies and baby things were in store in Tanganyika!

However, panic over – the crisis was resolved, the canal stayed open and I was able to come down from Moshi to meet them at Mombasa, drive back to Moshi and reunite Barbara with the nappies!

Moshi is situated on the southwestern slopes of Kibo, one of the two old volcanic peaks of Mount Kilimanjaro which rise from the surrounding plain. While Kibo is ice-capped, the other peak, Mawenzi, five miles to the east, is not and the two peaks are separated by the Saddle. The slopes of the mountain are very fertile and the Arabica coffee grown here by the Wa–Chagga tribe makes them one of the richest tribes in East Africa. Sugar cane and bananas are also important crops from this region.

*

Soon after we settled in at Moshi, Peter was born in Moshi Hospital on Boxing Day (a couple of weeks early – we blamed the brandy butter!). He weighed only three pounds eleven ounces at birth but, in spite of this poor beginning, he soon put on weight and began to flourish.

A little while later we were joined at Moshi by Ann and Dennis Dyer, just married and fresh from England. They were destined for Arusha, a town fifty miles to the west, but they had been posted to Moshi to gain some experience. They were staying in the Lion Cub Hotel just up the road from us and, while Dennis and I were out working, Ann came down to stay with Barbara.

We now had a more modern house with an inside kitchen complete with electric cooker, refrigerator and a washing machine. But we still had to resort to some traditional ways of doing things; like putting cans of water underneath the legs of the food storage cupboard to keep out the ants!

One morning, Ann was helping Barbara with the cooking when Barbara complimented her on the neat way she was preparing a kidney for a steak and kidney pie. Ann explained that her skills of precise dissection were learned when she was a medical student ... just before she gave that up to marry Dennis.

Soon after that, Barbara had another caller while I was out working asking if *Mr Truffle* was in. It turned out to be Ivor Hilliker who had just joined the Forestry Department to survey the boundaries of their Forestry Reserves. Ivor became a very good friend over the years but he never did learn to pronounce *Threlfall*!

*

In Moshi, there was rather more work involving safari - which, in Swahili, really means no more than 'journey' - than there had been in Dar es Salaam and Iringa which meant that everyone had to live in tents, take food supplies for a week, find a water supply etc. It was difficult for Barbara to come along with two small children but sometimes there was a nearby rest house we could use.

A couple of episodes stick in my mind from these times: we were once camped miles from anywhere and I had just dropped off to sleep when I heard a rustling in the tent. I switched on my torch and found myself amidst a column of safari ants on the move! I leapt out of bed, my legs badly bitten, and tottered off to where the gang were camped to seek help.

As I recall, we were camped close to an old ruined German house but had, for some reason, decided to use the tents for sleeping. We now rapidly changed our minds and moved the beds into the house for the rest of the night. In the morning the ants had all disappeared!

On another occasion I was driving the survey lorry, with all the gang aboard, down an isolated track called Thompson's Road. Half way between Kibo and Mt Meru we saw that a vehicle travelling in the opposite direction had stopped. The driver was taking aim at a lion on a kill a few hundred yards away. As we stopped, he shot again and killed the lion. To shoot big game like lions it was necessary to have a game permit and I assumed he had one.

We all disembarked and approached the lion with caution. My gang then helped him to put the lion in the back of his lorry. As we chatted, I learned that he was from Arusha, and that he had a bull terrier bitch who had just had a litter. He had some spare puppies and I knew Barbara would welcome a dog, partly for protection when I was away and partly for company so I said that, subject to her approval, we would take one of the puppies. And that is how we came to acquire Sally!

It was whilst I was in Moshi in March 1953 that I took the final examination for the A.R.I.C.S. (Associate of the Royal Institution of Chartered Surveyors) examination. My degree had exempted me from the intermediate exam but I had to go to Nairobi for a couple of days. I remember that Stalin died on one of the days I was there.

*

Susan started school while we were in Moshi, and Barbara used to walk to the school with her, accompanied by Peter in a pushchair with Sally on a lead.

Peter was baptised when he was a few months old by the Bishop of Central Australia who happened to be on safari in East Africa at the time.

*

One of the most interesting survey tasks I ever had to undertake was to help measure the height of Kibo in September 1952. The Germans had established the height using a primitive form of height determination called a boiling point thermometer and their result of 19,595 feet was generally used on maps of East Africa.

The more accurate method we used was to fix the horizontal position of Kibo by triangulation and then measure the difference in height between it and the known heights of two triangulation stations - Lelatema and Domberg - both about thirty miles to the south by reciprocal theodolite observations.

Each station was marked by a heliograph – a six-inch mirror which could be used to reflect the sun's rays from one station to another to provide a clear target over a long distance for theodolites on the other stations to focus on.

I camped overnight on one of the two southern stations, Mt Lelatema, so as to be ready to start observations in the morning. I set up the theodolite and the heliographs and awaited signals from Kibo and Domberg. Time passed … and passed … and passed … with no signal from the other stations. We had borrowed some radio transmitters and receivers from the King's African Rifles to enable us to keep in touch with each other but I became increasingly frustrated when I could not make any radio contact, so much so that I finally spoke into the microphone, 'If this is the Army signals system, thank Heaven we have a navy!'

Now, Barbara and Ann Dyer were sitting in our house in Moshi with our radio tuned to the army frequency and were very entertained when they heard my comment quite clearly. No-one else appeared to have heard it so I was saved from considerable embarrassment!

Soon after that, the bright lights from the other two heliographs became visible and the observations were made. Later calculations fixed the height of Kibo as 19,340 feet.

Several years later, when the Dyers had moved to the USA, a salesman called at their house to try to sell them a copy of the Encyclopaedia Britannica. Dennis looked through some of the volumes and came upon an article on Kilimanjaro which gave the height as 19,595 ft. He was not impressed!

Of all the memories from my fourteen years in Tanganyika, one of the clearest is of seeing a heliograph shining down from the summit of Kilimanjaro. I am therefore tempted to quote from a poem by the Romantic poet Leigh Hunt:

> *Say I'm weary, say I'm sad,*
> *Say that health and wealth have missed me,*
> *Say I'm growing old, but add ...*
> *I saw a bright light shining from the top of Africa's highest*
> *mountain!*

*

Our next door neighbours in Moshi had spent some time living in Italy and had thoroughly enjoyed it. They inspired us, when our next home leave was looming on the horizon, to consider travelling by ship to Italy and then by car through Europe to England. The thought became a plan and we were soon making definite arrangements.

We were entitled to first class passages from Tanganyika to England by ship or air, but we were allowed to take the cash equivalent and use it to arrange our own passage if we wished. There was an Italian shipping line, Lloyd Triestino, whose twin ships, the Africa and the Europa, plied between Trieste and Cape Town down the east coast of Africa calling at both Dar es Salaam and Mombasa. The cash allowance in lieu of our first class passage would comfortably cover return tourist class passages on a

Lloyd Triestino ship to Italy plus the freight charge for our car, so that is what we set about arranging.

Loading the Vanguard on the Africa 1954

Since Peter would be barely two and a half years old when we landed in Italy, and Susan about six, we decided it would be better to camp rather have to look for accommodation en-route so we spent a lot of time planning our equipment and working out how to stow it in the Vanguard.

We bought a small ridge tent about six feet long and five feet high with two small camp beds and sleeping bags for ourselves. Susan fitted quite easily on the back seat of the car, with Peter in the luggage space behind the back seat. For bedding, Barbara converted a double eiderdown which had been a wedding present (ideal for the tropics!) into two suitably-sized sleeping bags for the children. We had an x-pattern wash basin which, with the legs let down, converted into a camp bath or a camp table, as well as a pressure cooker and primus stove for cooking (using petrol for fuel rather than kerosene which would be less easily available).

We also acquired three old Shell petrol cans - the kind that 1920s touring cars carried on their running boards. We used one for petrol for the primus stove and two for water. The intention was to put all this gear into a packing crate which would travel in the hold of the Africa and then be loaded into the car when the ship arrived at Brindisi before we drove off. We rehearsed the routine of packing and unpacking this equipment, plus our own personal baggage, until we could almost do it in our sleep!

We armed ourselves with some basic spoken Italian with the help of our neighbour and a simple text book entitled 'Italian in Three Months Without a Master'; I suggested it might have been more interesting to have one called 'Italian in Three Months With a Mistress' but there didn't seem to be such a publication!

*

A few days before the date we were due to drive down to Mombasa and board the ship, we found that heavy rains had closed the road! What were we to do?

Tanganyika Railways had no passenger berths left on a suitable train but fortunately they did agree to put the car on the train and allow us to travel in it. So there we were, sleeping in the Vanguard facing backwards and awaking next morning in Mombasa's goods marshalling yards!

A visit from the Grays in Moshi, pictured with Susan and Peter

*

The Africa was a more modern ship than the two British ships we had previously sailed on and even the Tourist Class cabins were more comfortable than their First Class. Between each pair of Tourist Class cabins there was a shower room with a loo: when using it you had to remember to lock the door from the other cabin. On the British ships it had been necessary to go down in the bowels of the ship and bathe in salt water using a tablet of salt water soap. Imagine that with two children!

Also, the Africa was fully air-conditioned and a large carafe of wine was provided free with all meals in Tourist Class whereas First Class passengers had to buy wine by the bottle!

Drinks in the Africa saloon

We really enjoyed our trip on the Africa until a couple of days before we were due to arrive at Brindisi. Barbara was suddenly taken ill and was having rigors with a very high temperature. It was obviously malaria. She was taken into the sick bay where the treatment offered seemed to consist mainly of enemas! However, it seemed to work and when the time came to disembark she was feeling much better and ready to set off.

We waited on the quay whilst the car was offloaded together with our crate. I had brought with me in the car a hammer and a tool which, in Swahili, is called a 'kisuku', meaning very appropriately a 'parrot'. In English we would refer to it as a nail extractor.

The trick was to hammer the slot behind the head of the nail and then lever the nail out. Having taken the lid off the crate, we then followed our well-rehearsed routine putting every item in its appointed place in the car. When we had finished the empty crate sat forlornly on the quayside!

*

The weather in Brindisi was not at all suitable for camping – in fact, it was blowing a gale so we decided it would make much more sense to seek a roof over our heads. I am not sure how we found the house we did eventually spend the night in –possibly it was an address we had been given by a tourist office - but it certainly was quite an experience.

The local women's dress reminded us of African women's and they treated us as if we had just arrived from Mars; they even brought their friends to inspect the strange arrivals!

It was obviously a very poor part of Italy and definitely not a well-frequented tourist area. However, the locals were very friendly and helpful and they rustled up some clean bedding and a hearty meal consisting mostly of spaghetti. We were able to make use of our newly-acquired Italian, and we felt we had really made their day. Yet, in some ways, we felt we had not yet left Africa.

The next day, the weather had cleared and we pressed on through Bari to Naples. This was where we first encountered Italian camping sites and they were excellent - far superior to anything in England where you were lucky to find anything better than a farmer's field with a standpipe in the corner.

Here everything was efficiently organised, clean and tidy: showers, toilets, swimming pool, shop, etc., all clearly indicated by signs in four languages plus a sketch/symbol for the others. Some of the tents were quite elaborate and obviously expensive. We felt perhaps the owners preferred a good quality tent to the caravan a British camper might have bought, and perhaps climate was part of the reason.

While we were in Naples, we visited Pompeii, which was most impressive, and we bought a copy of the paving slab at the entrance to one of the houses saying CAVE CANEM. We still have it.

Peter soon tired of walking (not surprisingly) and I had to carry him some of the way. We also went up Mount Vesuvius and saw a very small parch of molten lava! Naples was also the first place we saw any signs of other English people – a British car bearing a GB plate. That apart, we might otherwise have been in a foreign country, which was how we preferred it.

From Naples we proceeded to Rome, where we stayed on a most attractive wooded campsite in the centre of the city. It was almost like staying on Hyde Park in London. This was where we first tasted yogurt and decided it went down better with a little added sugar.

Our most regular supper here, and in the rest of our journey through Italy, was spaghetti Bolognaise – spaghetti was easily obtainable and minced beef (macchinata) was available from the butcher. This meal was easily prepared in the pressure cooker, and was invariably followed by yogurt!

While in Rome, we walked round the forum, visited the Vatican, climbed up to the roof and saw the Pope.

After Rome, we spent a few days by the sea near Marina di Grosseto, a village right on the seaside near the town of Grosseto and directly opposite the island of Elba. The next village along the coast went by the lovely name of Castiglione della Pescaia. There was no official campsite at Marina di Grosseto but we set up our little camp under the pine trees a few yards from the sea. The site had few facilities but there were no people either – a very rural, restful existence.

Our camp on the beach at Marina di Grossetto

Every day or two we drove into Marina di Grosseto to wash our clothes at the village pump, refill our water cans at the village fountain and replenish our wine bottles at the 'Vini et Olio' shop. We had acquired quite a taste for Marsala.

At the weekend we met a family of four from Grosseto - mother, father, and two girls about Susan's age - who had just driven down for a few hours by the sea. The children got on very well and we had interesting conversations with the parents.

The man had obviously been in the Italian army during the war and he spoke about 'When I was with my tank in Africa'. He had also been a prisoner of war in Scotland and had acquired several appropriate phrases such as, 'Shut up!', 'Be Quiet!' and 'Stand Still!'. The latter phrase was also applied in Italian to the girls: 'Sta ferma!'

We were invited to visit them at their home which we did a few days later and were given a typically English afternoon tea (but Italian Style) – very weak with boiled milk which floated in lumps on the surface. But it was very kind of them to make the effort and we assured them that it was delicious!

Then up to Pisa with its Leaning Tower, the marble quarries at Carrara, the naval base at La Spezia and along the Italian Riviera to Genoa. I have two recollections of the camp site at Genoa: the first is of Barbara going to the camp shop and chatting with an Italian who, it transpired, had also been in a prisoner of war camp, this time in Kenya. Thus they were able to continue their conversation in Swahili! And the second is of going to bed at night and being kept awake for hours by two Nederland characters who seemed to be dismantling their Volkswagen Beetle to make two beds inside.

From Genoa, it was inland to Turin and another good campsite, then up the Dora Riparia valley into the Alps, over the Col de Montgenevre pass and down to Grenoble.

It was there that we discovered, while sorting out a few things on our roof rack, that we must have forgotten to replace our x-pattern washstand/bath at a stop en route. We thought it might be worthwhile to report our loss to a police station, which we did. Perhaps you can imagine what it is like explaining that we had just lost a bath whilst travelling over the Alps to a French police officer with a recruiting poster for the French Foreign Legion staring down at you from the wall!

We did not stay too long in France but headed through the Franche-Comte, crossed into Germany near Basel, and headed north into the Black Forest.

I forgot to mention earlier the formalities involved in taking a car through half a dozen different countries in Europe, each with its own Customs barriers.

Firstly, we had to obtain a large booklet containing a number of 'Triptiques' from the Automobile Association, each consisting of three detachable sections on which details of the car and its owner had to be entered. The first section was handed to the Customs Officer at the point of entry; thus they had a record that the car had entered the country without paying import duty. The second section was handed to Customs when the car left the country thus relieving the owner of the commitment to pay import duty.

In each case, the Customs Officer signed the third section of the tryptique, which stayed in the booklet. This meant, in theory, that if the car was badly damaged in an accident, the wreckage had to be exported to avoid paying duty! However, the system worked quite well apart from the delay at the Custom Posts on entering and leaving Italy, France, Germany, Belgium, Holland and Britain.

Our first main stop in Germany was at Freiburg-im-Breisgau, the capital of the southern Black Forest: a very pleasant, unspoiled old German town with typical German buildings including especially the cathedral - one of the most perfect specimens of Gothic architecture in Germany - and an old university (1457).

We spent one night at Wolfach, only a village but with a broad main street flanked by large gabled old German houses, and one night on our own, alone in the forest, trying to put all the old Grimm Brothers' horror stories out of our minds.

The road to the north sometimes ran along the western limit of the Black Forest overlooking the Rhine Rift Valley. The Vosges formed the western edge about twenty miles away and one was sometimes tempted off the main road by signs reading 'Blick am Rhein' (View over the Rhine) which here forms the boundary between France and Germany.

We next came to Heidelburg, situated on the River Neckar, a tributary of the Rhine - another old German university town (1385) whose huge ruined castle dominates the town and the bridge over the river.

Continuing north, we reached Bingen, about ten miles west of Mainz. There we entered the Rhine Rift Valley, approximately a mile across and overlooked by craggy peaks often crowned with old ruined castles and famous wine-making villages such as Bacharach, which we explored, confined only to the limited areas of flat land near the river.

I quote from Oz Clarke's 'Book of Wine': 'If you want fairytale castles, near vertical sheets of vineyard rising out of the tumbling river water, with picturesque gabled villages snuggling into the foot of the rock face, and the distant strains of the Lorelei maidens humming away in the depths of your imagination – then this is the place for you. But you'll have to remember that it's also the place for several million other like-minded tourists, all flocking in for the romance of the Rhine gorges, and the siren song of the Lorelei will get drowned in the clamour. Even so, this stretch of the Rhine valley between Bingen and Koblenz is intensely beautiful.'

But we were so lucky! The tourist trade had barely begun in 1954 and we were able to see and appreciate this, and so many other beautiful areas, in peace and quiet.

The Lorelei, by the way, is a steep rock rising out of the right bank of the river which was the home of maidens whose sweet song lured sailors to their doom on the rock.

After the Rhine Valley we visited Cologne where we saw the Cathedral, still supporting its distinctive twin towers even though it had been badly damaged during the latter stages of the war in 1945. Close to the west end of the cathedral, a bomb had made an enormous crater which had exposed a large and beautiful Roman pavement which remained unprotected. Indeed, driving into, and out of, Cologne, we found large areas of bomb damage which had still not been restored nine years after the war ended.

At Aachen (French 'Aix La Chapelle') we went into the cathedral which contains the tomb of Charlemagne. Travelling on, we bypassed Brussels, spent a little time in Bruges and then went straight to the hotel we had booked. It was just across the border in Holland in Cadsand Bad and was right on the coast.

Barbara's parents had arranged to come over to Ostend on the ferry, and we met them there. They had no suitcase with them but George was clutching a ticket he had been given to reclaim his case on board! So they had no case and Mrs H's only concern was to borrow a nightdress from Barbara for the night.

On leave in Elmdon, 1954

We managed to reclaim their case the next day and enjoyed several pleasant days by the seaside with a day or two spent in Bruges.

The children, as usual, soon fraternised with the locals and we slept - as we had been doing - in the tent with the children in the car. One morning we rather overslept and were accused by one of the locals of being (this is how the Flemish sounded) 'lousy langschlappers'.

*

At the end of this respite, we boarded the ferry to Dover and then drove up to Scunthorpe.

This particular leave we had taken care to ensure we had somewhere of our own to stay and had rented a thatched cottage in a little village called Elmdon, not far from Saffron Walden. Susan went to the village school and it was far easier to entertain visitors than be guests in someone else's house for the whole of our leave. We had Barbara's parents, Connie and George, Brenda and Geoff (Barbara's brother and his wife) and Ann and Dennis Dyer to stay for a few days (but not all at once).

One of our neighbours found a wasps' nest in her garden and George, an enthusiastic fisherman, was interested because apparently the larvae make good bait. He dug up the nest and put it in our little oven to kill off the wasps. The larvae were taken away in triumph to Scunthorpe.

This was not my only recent encounter with the apian species. On one occasion in Dar es Salaam, I was driving Emma back to the office after lunch one day when I became aware of a buzzing noise and noticed bees flying in and out of the car. I stopped and investigated and found that I had been sitting on a swarm of the little blighters in the wooden box under my seat! I took a chance and drove on to the office where I arranged for a pest control man to deal with my unwelcome residents.

*

At the end of our leave, about October time, we drove back across Europe by the quickest route to board the Africa at Venice. We had bought a few items to take back to Tanganyika and avoided purchase tax by having them delivered either to our car at Dover (a Kenwood food mixer and a set of Mappin and Webb cutlery) or to the ship at Venice (a Kemble piano which we had ordered during a visit to the factory in North London).

The voyage back to Dar es Salaam was pleasant but uneventful; Barbara and the children stayed in Dar with our friends Mary and Gordon Gray for about a week while the car was resprayed. The original paint was a metallic grey but it had become quite patchy and I had arranged to have it resprayed in a plain light grey colour.

On completion, Barbara arranged for it to be put on a flat wagon on the railway up to Tabora and she travelled with the children on the same train. I had taken an earlier train to Tabora without any delay in Dar to start a new training course for African would-be surveyors at Tabora School.

Although nothing official was ever said until Harold Macmillan's 'wind of change' speech in Cape Town, it must have been obvious that pressure was beginning to grow for decolonisation; a pressure which manifested itself in Kenya in the early 1950s during the violent Mau-Mau rebellion. Moshi was not very far from the Kenyan border and, during our stay there, Barbara had slept with a pistol under her pillow whenever I was on safari.

The Africans in Tanganyika had not generally reached a very high standard of education – a School Certificate was a rarity – and it must have been obvious that if independence was followed by an exodus of expatriate surveyors some steps ought to be taken to fill the gap, hence the modest start in Tabora.

The piano and other goods travelled up on the train with me and, on arrival at Tabora, I just managed to prevent the porters pushing the heavy piano straight from the floor of the wagon to the platform, a foot or more lower. There was a well-known story that Tanganyika Railways had once broken a blacksmith's anvil in transit, though I cannot vouch for the truth of it.

When I got the piano to the house, I thought I would just try it out but when I pressed the keys the sound was very muffled.

'Oh dear!' I thought. 'Damage!'

However, I was relieved to find that we had packed blankets inside and they were the cause of the muffled sound!

*

I was allocated one classroom in Tabora School, a secondary school for Africans, together with one pupil and was then left to my own devices. Susan was enrolled in the local European School and we settled down for a three-year tour of duty.

Tabora was not the most attractive of places; it was roughly in the middle of the country, on the main railway line between Dar es Salaam and Lake Tanganyika, with a rail connection to Mwanza on Lake Victoria to the north.

However, it was not to be a three-year tour. After a few weeks I received a message that my immediate superior, Doug Warren, who was working in the survey administration in Dar es Salaam, had broken his leg and I was ordered to come down and take over from him. So, in February 1955, we all had to pack again and go down to Dar es Salaam, with the prospect of yet another school for Susan.

Doug Warren's official title was Superintendent of Surveys (Headquarters), abbreviated to SS(HQ), with responsibility, under the Director of Surveys (ex-Chief Surveyor) for all the work in the office – checking surveys and the drawing and printing of maps and plans, of which I had never had much experience.

And the Chief Surveyor (sorry ... Director of Surveys!) was Norman Guy, who knew quite a lot about map making which made life rather difficult for me, especially as he was quite a dominating character. Added to which the Chief Printer was Bert Price who was quite an uncooperative Bolshie trade union type from the East End. So 1955 was not the happiest year of my career in Tanganyika. But we got by.

*

A few months into 1956, Doug Warren recovered and I was posted to Tanga, about 120 miles up the coast from Dar es Salaam. For the first few months there was some normal cadastral surveying to be done and then I had to finish off the demarcation of the Kenya-Tanganyika boundary.

My predecessor in Tanga had made a start from the coast about forty miles north of Tanga and I had to carry on the demarcation for about fifty miles in a northwesterly direction towards Kilimanjaro; from there the work would be taken over by the Survey of Kenya. The country we had to work through was well wooded and undulating; our specification was to cut a trace forty feet wide and to place intervisible beacons throughout the length. The cylindrical beacons were about four feet high and one foot across and were formed by filling a metal case with concrete and supporting it with a substantial block of concrete in the ground. The survey work was simple – having once established the bearing it could easily be carried forward and observations using triangulation points in the Usambara Mountains to the west served to keep us on course.

But it was the logistical aspects of the work that were the most challenging. These included:

(a) Cutting the trace: we soon found that the trees, though not very large, were extremely hard and our axes were not up to the job. I had to indent for some two-handed saws which were much more effective. This work was very labour-intensive but there were no villages in the area. However, we managed to recruit about twenty local tribesmen (Wakamba, I think) to supplement my normal staff of about ten.

(b) Water supply: there was no water close to the trace and every few days our lorry had to drive ten to twenty miles to the nearest river to refill our forty gallon drums which we needed not only for drinking and cooking but also for making concrete for the beacons. One very hot day we set off in the lorry to build another beacon. No sooner was the water drum offloaded than the workers made to have a drink. I was not very popular when I made them wait until we had mixed the concrete for the beacon!

(c) Food supply: all our provisions had to be fetched from Tanga in the Land Rover and I soon found that we were being asked to bring inordinate amounts of sugar. These quantities were greatly reduced when it became clear that the locals were using it to brew 'pombe' - the native beer.

We soon developed a routine of moving camp when it became uneconomical to make a daily return trip to the end of the cut trace and this was our life for a few weeks.

Barbara and Peter were with me most of the time and Susan during school Christmas holidays. Barbara soon found herself holding morning sick parades, patching up minor injuries and dispensing basic remedies to our labour force.

I had an assistant surveyor with me, Rene Vidot, a Seychellois whose French accent was most reminiscent of Charles Boyer! It was he who showed us the first coco de mer which is native to the Seychelles.

Rene's bushcraft was remarkable. One day, we were driving in the Land Rover when we had a puncture. We had a spare wheel, a jack and a wheel brace but it was quite impossible to slacken the wheel nuts. Rene collected some dry grass and twigs on top of a flat stone and located a hollow plant stem similar to a drinking straw. This 'blowpipe' served to direct the flame from the burning tinder on to a wheel nut and the heat expansion soon made it possible to turn the nuts and change the wheel.

Peter with elephant tusks on the Kenya-Tanganyika border, 1957

He was also an excellent shot and our dinners of impala fillet kebabs round the campfire were amazingly memorable.

The African cook we had with us was quite well educated and after dinner opinions would be expressed about the possibility of independence for Tanganyika. I remember the coup de grace Rene delivered to end the discussion one evening: 'Do not forget, Stephen, that fifty years ago your grandfather was eating missionaries!' The veracity was doubtful but the effect was certainly conclusive!

One day, driving back to camp, we noticed a flock of vultures hovering some distance away. We left the track to investigate and found a dead elephant. There were no obvious signs of injury and we assumed it had either died of natural causes or poison. We cut out the tusks and later, in accordance with regulations, handed them in to the Government Office.

We finally reached the end of the line. I fixed the position on the edge of a valley and, down below, we could clearly see a herd of elephants making its way slowly through the trees. I would have liked to put in the final beacon but it was clear that darkness would fall before we had finished and the gang were clearly worried that there might be other game around as well as the elephants. I put it to them that if I was willing to stay they should do the same.

'Yes, bwana,' said the headman. 'But you smell!'

I am sure this was not intended as a reflection on my personal hygiene but came from their belief that there was some aura about me, which they did not possess, which rendered me immune to attack. There was no answer to that so we cut a substantial peg from a tree branch and hammered it in flush with the ground, intending to replace it with a beacon the next day.

We returned the following morning to find that our king-sized peg had been pulled up by the elephants! We replaced it with a beacon but I had grave doubts that it, too, would soon succumb to a peevish attack by the elephants. We regularly found evidence that beacons were being damaged by elephants and I fear they were not substantial enough to survive for very long. Equally, it was likely that natural regeneration would soon obliterate our forty-foot wide cut through the forest. Perhaps some day an archaeologist will relocate the boundary and say, 'Ah, well! It was a good effort!'

Away from the boundary, one small but amusing incident in Tanga has remained in my mind: I had my theodolite on Point A and wanted to sight on Point B a short distance away … but there was an African house on the line.

As African houses were made of mud and wattle and were easily repaired the owner had no objection to my cutting holes in the two walls to sight through. While doing so I had a look inside the house and found an electric light bulb suspended from the ceiling by a piece of string. There was no electricity supply for miles and one imagines he had seen light bulbs in more substantial houses and had hoped his bulb would illuminate by magic.

But stranger still – on a shelf on the wall he had a spare bulb!

Susan was now at school at Lushoto – she started on 16th May 1955
while we were in Dar es Salaam, going up by bus with her 'Naafi spanner' round her neck.

We are sure she did not really enjoy it and her particular bete noire was the matron, Miss Buckle. But, at least, she was settled.

In Tanga, Peter went to a mission school just along the road and was taught by Sister Muriel, a lovely lady. Our house in Tanga was an old German building with a verandah all round, very suitable in a hot climate.

Sally was very much at home there. When Barbara came across a suitable mate for her, she had a fine litter of seven puppies.

Susan waiting to board the bus in Dar es Salaam which took her to school in Lushoto

*

We flew down to Dar es Salaam and spent an enjoyable Christmas with Ann and Dennis Dyer. The 'survey school' I had started in Tabora with one pupil had moved down to Dar with a few more trainees and was now run by Dennis.

While we were in Tanga, Princess Margaret came out to Tanganyika to open the new deep water berths in Dar es Salaam harbour and she also paid a visit to Tanga. I forget what it was that she came for, but there was to be some sort of ceremony and we had an invitation to attend, as also had Ivor Hilliker - now stationed near Susan's school with his lovely new wife, Sylvia - and also Susan's headmaster, Mr Smith, and his wife. And Susan came down as well.

The Hillikers stayed overnight with us; the Smiths came down at the crack of dawn and came to our house to change. They all had breakfast with us, which made a sitting of eight in all and we had about half an hour to eat breakfast before getting ready to go.

The first course we had was a slice of pawpaw (rather like melon) which needed to have sugar added before eating. There was only one sugar basin on the table and, as luck would have it, Ivor took it first and then started telling a story about something that had recently happened to him.

Now, Ivor was a lovely fellow but even his best friend would have had to describe him as slow. With the sugar basin in one hand and the spoon in the other he went through his story, pausing now and then to make a point, until eventually the sight of everyone peering at their watches must have hit home and the sugar basin was finally passed on! We arrived at the ceremony just in time!

The ceremony involved, apart from anything else, Princess Margaret's being driven slowly around the arena so that the assembled crowd could see her and she could wave to them. This is the only time I ever heard African women ululating in greeting a visiting important person – a high-pitched note interrupted by rapid tongue movement.

I later learned that the accelerator in the police Land Rover (in which she was being driven round the arena) had been adjusted to keep the vehicle moving at a slow and steady speed considered suitable for the occasion. But soon after the circuit began Princess Margaret demanded that they drive faster! She did not make a very favourable or lasting impression in Tanga!

One of the jobs I had to do during our time in Tanga was to check the survey of an estate at Pangani - at the mouth of the Pangani River. There was a rest house there so it was easy to take the family - Barbara, Peter and Sally with her litter of puppies. And Cat!

The previous occupant of the rest house had obviously been desperate to get away because the on walls of the living room were written in large letters '... 105 days to leave ...104 days ... 103 days' etcetera! I cannot remember whether it came down to '0 days'.

The survey was on the far side of the river and I had to take the lorry every morning, with my equipment and the gang, across on the ferry which had to struggle against the strong river current. But I believe the whole extended family enjoyed the break from Tanga.

*

In the Spring of 1957 we were due for leave again and once more booked a return trip on the Africa. We sold the Vanguard in Tanga and ordered a VW Beetle to be delivered in London.

There was no direct railway line between Tanga and Mombasa so we had to take the train up to Moshi where we were re-united with some of our old friends. From there we travelled into Kenya to Voi junction and down to Mombasa.

I forgot to mention earlier we had bought a colour cine-camera in Tanga and had been able to record much of our life there, as well as the voyage home and the leave that followed. I particularly remember the voyage through the Suez Canal, passing the Greek Islands at dawn and Peter feeding the pigeons in St Mark's Square.

From Venice we took the Orient Express to London and I recall clearly, when we retired to our bunks, saying 'Buona Notte!' to the cabin attendant but greeting the same man the next morning with 'Bon Jour!' because we were now in France!

On arrival in London we went to stay for a few days with my brother Cedric and his wife Ellen in Wallingford, and picked up the VW Beetle in London. We then went on a mini-tour of England – Hampton Court, Stonehenge, Ferndown (where we visited my father's brother, my Uncle Harvey, Aunt Minnie and Cousin Roland), the New Forest, Exmoor, Looe, Porlock, Cheddar Gorge and, finally, a few days in Scunthorpe.

During this tour, we collected Susan at Heathrow when she came from Lushoto School at the end of term. We spent the rest of our leave at a cottage we had rented at Woolpit, near Bury St Edmunds, and then we all four set off in the VW with a new larger tent to accommodate all four of us as there would not be room for the children in the VW when we returned to Tanganyika.

Across the Channel from Dover to Calais, then quickly across France to Heidelberg; south to Lake Constance and Zurich where I visited the Wild theodolite factory at Heerbrug; south to the attractive old town of Schwyz, then to Interlaken and on the mountain railway up to the peak of the Jungfrau at 4,148 metres.

There is an observatory at the top and the children were able to ride on a dog sled some way down the Aletsch Glacier ... and back! This building has since been enlarged to accommodate about a dozen restaurants and other facilities for the flood of (mainly Japanese) tourists who now swamp the mountain.

There was an early fall of snow during the night and our crossing of the Grimsel Pass was difficult. I had to help push the car in front so that we could carry on climbing. We crossed the Simplon Pass (there is now a tunnel) and drove down into the warmth of Italy. From there we went to Stresa on Lake Maggiore, south to the Mediterranean, and then to Rome where we took Susan to the airport. An air hostess walked her across the tarmac to board the plane back to school.

Our most enduring memories of Rome are, firstly, of Peter attempting to follow tradition by throwing a coin over his shoulder into the Trevi fountain. He failed miserably! It landed somewhere near his feet. Then there was the visit into the hill station of Tivoli to the Villa d'Este with its hundreds of fabulous fountains.

After that, we had to turn towards Trieste to rendezvous with the Africa. We passed through Siena and its Piazza del Campo, the site of the annual Palio - the dangerous horse race round the piazza. Then to Florence where we spent a day or two exploring the city and finally to Trieste with a day in the gardens of Miramare and an anxious ten minutes watching the VW being hoisted up into the hold of the Africa.

When we checked in with our tickets, we were regarded with awe when I said that this was 'nostro quarto viaggio nel Africa.' It seemed as if they were admiring our resilience! The advantage of sailing from Trieste was that we then had two or three free days in Venice in our floating hotel.

The most memorable incident during this voyage was that off the coast of Somaliland, in the late evening, we met the Africa's sister ship, the Europa, northbound for Italy. Both ships put on their full lights and sounded their sirens and generally said, "How very nice to meet you!"

From 1957 onwards I was stationed at Headquarters in Dar es Salaam, either as SS(HQ) or for a time as Acting PAS (Principal Assistant Secretary). One of the changes I introduced during that time was to the drawing and printing methods.

One of the great drawbacks to using paper for drawing and printing is that it is very vulnerable to great changes in humidity and temperature in the tropics. If maps are printed in, say, four colours and the colour separation sheets for these expand or contract differently, then the detail in each colour will not be in quite the right position relative to the detail in the other colours – there will be what is termed a 'lack of registration'.

I went up to discuss this with the man in charge of drawing and printing in the Uganda Survey Department and learned about new methods which used a plastic material called Astralon - which did not expand or contract like paper. To make everything official, he came down to Dar es Salaam, inspected our methods and wrote a report recommending the improvements ... which did not go down well with the 'set-in-their-ways' printers but were implemented nonetheless.

*

Our very pleasant house at Oyster Bay had a large outcrop of coral in the garden – the remains of an old reef left high and dry when the sea level fell. We enlarged the cavities in it to make flower beds and produced a very attractive rock garden.

We also acquired two pet guinea pigs from the hospital which were, they assured us, both female. But when we found a very small addition one morning, we began to have our doubts! Mother and father were given the names of Margaret and George and their newly-arrived son was called Buster. They were allowed out of the hutch quite a lot and the parents used to follow Peter round the garden in Indian file while Buster fitted very comfortably in the pocket of his shorts.

Our two rabbits - Lettuce and Tomato - also had the run of the garden. Their fur was very light coloured and when it rained Barbara used to bath them and dry them on her knee with her hair dryer. Sally and Cat also enjoyed the freedom of the garden so it vaguely resembled a Game Reserve!

Sadly, Barbara's mother died in October 1957. Not having a telephone, we did not find out until a week afterwards.

*

It became clear about this time that independence for Tanganyika was much closer than anyone had dreamed possible a couple of years beforehand and the awful word 'Tanganyikanisation' was coined - meaning the replacement of European staff by native Tanganyikans. Things were obviously going to change and everyone started to wonder how it would affect them.

Peter and Susan were both reaching the age where we would have to think about their future schooling. There were prep and secondary schools in Tanganyika and Kenya but it seemed more sensible to look further ahead and find a school in England for them. We had taken exploratory steps when we visited England in 1957 and by 1960 we had Susan booked into the East Anglian School for Girls with Peter pencilled in to join the associated Culford School for Boys – both close to Bury St Edmunds.

Barbara flew home on leave in June - a few weeks before me - to kit the children out for the beginning of term. The outfitter for both schools was Joshua Taylor in Cambridge and she had to spend a small fortune buying all the necessary gear.

Peter's new clothing included a winter overcoat; this for an eight-year-old boy who had never in his life worn anything more than a pair of thin shorts and sometimes a short-sleeved shirt. He was helped on with this garment ... and slowly sank to his knees, overcome by the weight!

They stayed in Cambridge for a day or two with Cliff Smith (of the pontoon school in 1946/7) and his wife, Margaret. All three then went to stay with Barbara's father at 59 West Common Lane, Scunthorpe, and I joined her soon afterwards. We stayed there until the beginning of term in September and then took the children down to their schools.

We thought it might be in order to take George for a little holiday to cheer him up so we hired a car and booked a ferry out of Folkestone. The night before crossing the Channel, we stayed in a guest house in the town and later found out that George had been spinning a hard luck story to the landlady. Apparently we had only packed coffee in our daily cuppa box but he had to have his cup of tea! So she gave him enough tea bags to tide him over. And did he enjoy them! In fact, I think he really enjoyed the whole trip because the only other occasion he had been out of England was when he crossed the Channel to meet us in Belgium in 1954.

Three episodes stick in my mind from this little tour.

We went as far east as the Grossglockner Pass (c.2500m.) and Barbara and George had a snowball fight by the roadside.

We stayed in one gasthof and had steak for supper. George had never seen such an enormous piece of steak before so he extracted a folding two-foot wooden rule from his jacket pocket and proceeded to measure the dimensions of the steak. He then took a note book from another pocket and wrote the dimensions within. He explained that he had to do this or his mates at work would never believe him!

One day we came to Igls, near Innsbruck, and drove up a mountain track which finally came to an abrupt end. The slope was such that it was clearly impossible to turn the car without it falling over on its side so what were we to do?

A sturdy Austrian farmer and his equally sturdy wife were working nearby raking up the hay so I rapidly brushed up my German and approached him with, "Koennen Sie uns helfen, bitte?" simultaneously indicating the car. The kind of help needed was pretty obvious: he called to his wife, a little way away, in a tone that brooked no refusal, "Else!

Kommen Sie!"

Else kommen pretty smartly and the pair of them applied their considerable weight to one side of the car whilst I edged it slowly round. Brute force had saved the day! We thanked them profusely (they refused any present) and we drove down the hill rejoicing. George no doubt recorded that incident with his steak size reminiscence.

*

When we were back at West Lane, George, completely out of the blue, suddenly said, 'Do you think I could come out to Tanganyika to see you?'

His appetite for foreign travel had obviously been whetted and we assured him he would always be very welcome. It so happened that our friends, Ivor and Sylvia Hilliker, would be returning from leave about the time he had in mind and we arranged a passage for him on their ship in late October which sailed through Suez.

On his arrival we went aboard to greet him and I remember standing with him watching the African stevedores unloading the freight from the hold with a great deal of shouting and gesticulation. George's laconic comment after a few minutes was, 'They're a rum lot, aren't they?'

A year or two before this, Barbara had started working for the Port Employers' Association and had acquired a black VW Beetle to take her to work. She left the ignition key in the kitchen so that the shamba boy, when he arrived, could clean the windscreen for the memsahib to go to work. One morning, while I was attending a conference in Kampala, she went into the kitchen and found some of the shutters were wide open. She quickly realised that her car was missing. She came back into the bedroom to tell George and he asked why she had been into his bedroom during the night. She assured him she hadn't stirred all night.

George said, 'You must have because I looked at my watch to check the time' and bent down to pick up his watch. But it wasn't there!

It was not Barbara who had been into his bedroom but a thief.

Barbara immediately telephoned the police and a sergeant arrived shortly afterwards to take a statement and make a list of the missing items.

Later, an inspector came and went through the list. He particularly wanted to know more about the brandy which had been stolen. Brandy? Barbara looked at the list and found it included a brand-new watch. (George had recently treated himself to a new timepiece in Dar es

Salaam!)

The police soon recovered the car, undamaged, just a few miles away. They had less success catching the thief ... or finding the *brandy* new watch.

*

The rush towards independence had accelerated during the past year and suddenly we found that the 9th December 1961 was to be Independence Day ... or 'Uhuru' in Swahili.

When the time arrived, the Duke of Edinburgh was there to hand over whatever it is that colonial powers do hand over to newly independent states. I had obtained tickets for two seats at Dar es Salaam Airport to witness the Duke's arrival in an aircraft of the Queen's Flight but Barbara nobly sacrificed her ticket so that George could be there.

His Excellency the Governor together with all the local notables and government officials were lined up to greet the Duke as a body of the King's African Rifles marched smartly into position. The Duke stepped from the aircraft and walked over to greet the welcoming party. He was then was driven away accompanied by a cortege of motor cars. All very impressive!

Next day there was a garden party in the grounds of Government House which Barbara and I attended. The Duke was led round to greet various people stationed at strategic points and I was able to get some good video shots. I found it was the hats that impressed me most: all the tribal leaders - including Jomo Kenyatta - were wearing their tribal headdresses with exotic feathers and I swear they were more decorative than the hats some of the ladies had conjured up for the occasion. But it was a close run thing!

The formal handover of the keys to the kingdom took place at midnight with the usual lowering of the Union flag and the raising of the new Tanganyika flag. This was followed by a firework display.

The following day (Sunday) there was an official church service in St Alban's Church attended by Prince Philip and the Governor. Barbara sang in the choir and George was in the congregation. I waited outside with the press to take photographs as they all emerged.

And that was Uhuru. Tanganyika was now an independent country with its own president, Julius Nyerere, and the time had come to think about leaving Tanganyika to its own devices.

*

Soon after Uhuru, the British Government brought out a scheme of compensation for expatriate staff who wished to resign. They were to be awarded a lump sum plus their earned pension up to date. This meant I should be leaving with quite a lot of money ... but with no job to go to! I started to make enquiries and actually applied for a job teaching maths at a grammar school in Wiltshire. I was offered the post and accepted.

Then another post was offered which I considered was better suited and more attractive in the Cartographic Department of the Oxford University Press. I wrote to accept this and sent a 'deeply regret' letter to the grammar school.

So around the July of 1962 I handed in my letter of resignation to the government, we held a farewell party for all our friends at a restaurant, and we flew back to England.

Chapter 7: Oxford

We rented a house in North Oxford from a university don who was going away for six months and I started work at the OUP in St Giles.

It was never a really happy working environment and some of the people who had worked there for quite a long time followed one of their number to set up a cartographic department at Pergamon Press (owned by the now infamous Robert Maxwell) in the eastern suburbs of Oxford.

I decided to join them, starting in January 1963 at the beginning of the worst winter for years. Snow covered the ground until Easter!

After a few months I again decided that cartography alone was not for me so after completing a term as a supply teacher at Woodstock I decided to study for a Diploma in Education (Dip.Ed.) at the Department of Education in Oxford. I found this was quite stimulating and enjoyable.

I was attached to Worcester College, the sister college to St Catharine's, and I had no trouble finding a post at Banbury Grammar School in September 1964 where I taught Geography throughout the school and presented a mixed curriculum to one of the first year forms.

In the meantime we had bought (for less than £7,000!) an attractive old Victorian house on Cumnor Hill complete with half an acre of garden. I say 'attractive' but perhaps it should be 'potentially attractive' because it had been rather neglected and needed a couple of years t.l.c. to make it realise its potential, including burning off dark brown paint from the eight-inch deep elaborately-fashioned skirting boards. This was Barbara's job whilst I was teaching and a very dreary job it was!

Barbara's father had now come to live with us and he was delighted when the newly-installed warm air central heating system went a bit haywire as it made his bedroom very much hotter than the downstairs rooms. I seem to remember it reached the figure of ninety degrees Fahrenheit on one occasion!

Barbara joined the Oxford Bach Choir – to take her mind off the skirtings, I think – and discovered that Mrs Godden and her daughter, Sonnica, who were well-known breeders of German Shepherd dogs, lived just up the road. She had always wanted to own a G.S.D. and decided to earn some extra money so that she could buy one from the Goddens.

She was introduced to an Australian Professor of Old Testament Studies who wanted someone to take dictation and do some typing for him. She took the job and her salary helped to buy Shandy in May 1964.

Then she became Clerk to the Cumnor Parish Council for a year and seemed to be endlessly writing letters about the Swinford Toll Bridge and the planned Cumnor By-Pass. She eventually decided it would make more sense to get a job connected with schools so that we could have holidays together and set out to become a qualified teacher.

Westminster Teacher Training College was not far away and she started a course there in September 1965, leaving with her Teaching Certificate in 1968. She taught at nearby Cassington village school for one year, and then spent another year at the local Cumnor Village School.

*

In the meantime we had decided Shandy should have a companion and bought Flora from the Goddens in June 1966. Shandy had her first litter in May 1967 and this was the start of Barbara's breeding career. She registered the kennel name of Cumnorhurst with the Kennel Club and during the next thirty-five years she bred eighty-six litters, mostly from Flora and her descendants.

A few went into the police but most went to pet homes, and the prospective owners underwent a strict cross-examination to ensure that they were suitable. For example, it was unlikely that she would sell a puppy to a couple who were both in full time work because the animal would lack human contact during the day. Nor would she sell two male puppies to one family because it was very likely that jealousy could well lead to animosity resulting in the two of them fighting.

Breeding is not a profitable business unless you are fairly ruthless, get rid of a bitch when her breeding days are over, and sell puppies without enquiring into the background of the customer. Normally a bitch can only be used for breeding between the ages of two and seven years which means she is a 'passenger' for half of her life. But if you really care for your dogs you maintain this type of 'social security' where the 'workers' - i.e. the breeding bitches - pay for the upkeep of the youngsters and the 'pensioners'. This means you usually have to have four or five dogs in the house at one time which is no problem if they are well trained.

Finding a stud dog with suitable characteristics needs a great deal of consideration. Barbara bred mostly for character and temperament, not for shape, but unfortunately most stud dogs were also show dogs where shape was everything in the show ring.

It was the rule that a bitch in season had to be taken to the stud dog for mating and this often meant a drive of hundreds of miles with a return trip if she happened to get the wrong day when the bitch was not ready. The gestation period was about nine weeks but most bitches were a day or two early and one had to keep an eye on her for the tell-tale signs, get her into the whelping box, and help her as necessary.

The 'whelping box' was about four feet square with six inch high sides and had a two-inch square rail round the interior to prevent the bitches crushing any puppy which found its way between her back and the side of the box. Bitches often seemed to prefer to whelp about bedtime which meant Barbara spent a night on a camp bed by the side of the box.

*

We became involved in the church in Cumnor. I was on the PCC and Barbara and Susan sang in the choir. Barbara also played the organ when required.

The house next door to the church had been the home of Amy Robsart, the wife of Robert Dudley, Earl of Leicester, who became Queen Elizabeth the First's favourite in the 1550s. In 1560 Amy Robsart met her death by falling down a flight of stairs. It was a case of 'Did she fall or was she pushed?' If so, by whom?

Once we were settled in Oxford, Susan was moved to the local Matthew Arnold School and Peter to Magdalen College School near Magdalen Bridge and Magdalen College. His school blazer was black with red edging and when he first started at the school we had not yet redecorated the house. Most of the walls, including the staircase, had been covered in whitewash by the previous owners. When Peter came downstairs every morning, he naturally leaned against the wall all the way down so one of us had to stand at the bottom with a clothes brush to make him decent to go out.

Susan was married early in 1967 and Annette was born in December 1967. Alison was born in August 1969.

As for my own teaching career, Banbury was scheduled to become a comprehensive school in September 1967 and I moved to Oxford High School which, in turn, was then threatened with comprehensive status in September 1970!

I began to feel that I couldn't go on chasing grammar schools round the country indefinitely and after a family discussion we decided we might strike out and do something for ourselves. This meant waiting until Peter had taken his A-level examinations in June 1970 but in the meantime we examined the possibilities.

We had a small caravan at Cumnor Hill and I suggested buying a caravan site but Barbara pointed out that I would not be very happy at the end of the season repairing all the equipment the campers and caravanners had damaged. Nonetheless, we went to the Camping and Caravanning Exhibition at Earl's Court.

On the way, we bought a copy of *Our Dogs* on Paddington Station and found a number of advertisements in it for boarding kennels. This took Barbara's fancy immediately and I went along with the idea. Our only concern was that we had no experience of boarding kennels but after looking at some of the properties on sale, we decided we didn't need to worry too much. It was just a matter of a feeling for dogs plus common sense.

The properties varied from a few kennels in the back garden of a semi-detached house to the one we eventually bought which was four fields covering twelve acres, with a variety of animal houses and sheds converted into kennels. As in the case of 113 Cumnor Hill, it was scruffy and disorganised but the potential was there. We decided to buy it for £15,000.

I resigned from Oxford High School - almost driving the headmaster mad by leaving it till the last minute … just to be on the safe side!

Chapter 8: Enborne Kennels

Enborne Kennels was owned by Mr and Mrs Giddings and was really a smallholding where Mr Giddings kept cattle. His daughter, Marjorie, had started taking in dogs as boarders to help out a nearby boarding kennels when they were full. As a result, she had gradually built up her own clientele and had adapted some of the cattle sheds as kennels and bought some additional small dog kennels.

There were one or two dilapidated runs but for exercise the dogs were mostly walked on leads up the road three times a day, with help from schoolchildren at weekends and during school holidays. There were four grass fields in all but the boarding kennels were all concentrated in one field in which the house was also built. The other fields were rented out to other farmers until the property was sold.

When we came to examine the books and met some of the clients, it soon became obvious that boarding was not limited to school summer holidays as it had been with most of the other kennels we had visited. This was an all-year-round business with owners boarding their dogs when, for example, they went skiing or when a bitch was in season twice a year. This meant there was a steady annual income.

However, there were several other problems which would have to be resolved.

To start with, there was very little security. Taking a dog out of a kennel with a solid door (which prevents your seeing him) and trying to put a lead on him is just inviting the dog to rush past you. If a dog did this, there was no fence or gate behind you to prevent his escaping completely. In fact, this is exactly what happened soon after we took charge: this particular dog had come from London and was in a small wooden kennel. When Barbara opened the kennel door to put a lead on him he dashed past her and disappeared.

We drove round the roads in the vicinity but there was no sign of him and we had a very sleepless night. But when we went down to the kennels in the morning, there he was … sitting in his kennel!

The kennel area was about a hundred yards from the house and there was a cold water tap in one block only. The cattery was close to the house but the fish used to feed the cats was stored in a freezer in one of the kennel blocks. During the course of a day, sufficient fish for the number of residential cats was brought up to the house, defrosted and cooked, naturally spreading its aroma through the house. It was then taken down to the kennel block, put into dishes on a tray and carried up to the cattery.

The cattery had a very narrow corridor so that, carrying a tray, one had to walk sideways to pass down it. Later, the empty dishes were collected and taken down to the kennel block to be washed up in water heated in a large electric kettle. All extremely labour-intensive!

The cattery block itself was a Heath Robinson nightmare. The corridor in the cattery was roughly paved with broken paving stones but the floor of the pens was just rough concrete, very difficult to keep clean. The pitched roof of the cattery, made of corrugated asbestos, came down to within about a foot of the ground along the outside of the building, thus allowing free circulation of exterior air within the cattery.

The gap was covered with wire mesh which was splendid during warm weather but not during the winter. In bad weather, there were small wooden panels to close up these gaps and these had to be fitted whilst crawling along the outside of the building. The snag was that the gaps and the panels were of varying sizes and the panels had to be juggled about to find one to fit a certain gap whilst lying or kneeling on the ground at the foot of the roofing panel. Not a cattery design to be recommended! So the modus operandi had to be changed and the cattery had to be rebuilt - both part of one project.

One small feature of the property purchase we shall never forget was that in the kitchen was a smallish wall cupboard which was clearly a 'fixture or fitting' and hence part of the house. Mrs Giddings said that, if we wanted it, it would cost us ten pounds! We were too flabbergasted to argue. We were even more flabbergasted when she said the linoleum in the kitchen was glued down and could not be removed so we would have to buy that for sixteen pounds! I'm convinced she probably kept all her money in an old sock under the bed.

*

During the morning of the last Friday in July 1970, we were all at our separate schools on the last day of term - always a very busy time. In the afternoon we were with Marjorie Giddings receiving the dogs whose owners were just going away on summer holidays – an even busier time!

Marjorie stayed with us for a week or two to get us 'run in' and then we were on our own ... but not quite. Peter stayed with us until he went to Manchester University at the end of September; Margaret, who had a horse Nicky in one of the fields, and one or two schoolgirls agreed to come and work for us in the mornings during the holidays and somehow we managed to keep our heads above water until the rush had died down. Then we could start reorganising the whole set up.

It is difficult now to remember the exact order in which work was carried out but I will do my best!

As soon as residential numbers started to go down, we emptied one of the blocks and Peter, Barbara and I set about demolishing it. Peter climbed up on the roof and extracted all the spring nails which secured the asbestos roofing panels so that these could be removed leaving just the wooden framework and the corrugated iron walls which were the next to be taken off. Then Peter fastened ropes to the ridge timber and we all pulled on these until the whole structure collapsed sideways. We made an enormous bonfire of the wooden framework and the straw which had been put inside the walls to give some insulation (and which was tunnelled with rat runs!)

We contacted Cotswold Buildings, who manufactured prefab garages using large concrete panels with an attractive stone effect on the outside, and ordered an outsize garage about thirty feet long which would fit nicely in the space we had just created. Since it was prefabricated, it was essential that the dimensions of the concrete base which was laid had to be correct almost to a millimetre.

When the walls were in place, we had them all painted with white emulsion. A space was partitioned off at one end to serve as a kitchen and was fitted out with a sink, an electric water heater and cupboards. The concrete base was, of course, level and we had to have a smooth sloping granolithic concrete floor added so that any water used for washing down the kennels could find its way down the central corridor to the drain at the end.

The individual kennel partitions consisted of rigid galvanized steel mesh panels which bolted together to form the kennel sides with a gate panel to the central corridor. The kennels were either three or four feet wide, with one measuring five feet for extra large dogs. Barbara and I fixed all the panels ourselves and this, for me, brought back memories of my Meccano days!

Next, we had a suspended ceiling of plastic-faced plaster board fitted for insulation with strip lights illuminating the central corridor, individual infra-red heaters on adjustable chains above each bed space and a large exterior flood light on the roof.

The beds that Marjorie provided for the dogs were just piles of old clothing – blankets, sheets, shirts, woollies, and so forth which, of course, needed washing. In fact, when we first arrived, the kennel area resembled a gypsy encampment with all these scraps of material hanging out to dry!

We set to work on a number of sheets of blockboard and made a wooden bed consisting of a base and a front to fit in each kennel, painted either orange or blue. I later had to screw a strip of Dexion angle iron to the top of the upright to prevent the dogs from chewing it. Finally, we paved an area to the side of the kennel block and erected more mesh panels to form small runs. We also drained a larger area beyond those to accommodate six large runs, each about thirty feet by fifteen, four of

General view of Enborne Kennels

them grass, and two of gravel on a hard core base. This block was henceforth referred to as 'Cotswold' and marked the transition from Heath Robinson to Savoy Hotel!

All this work, which also provided the security of a closed gate behind you when you opened a kennel door, was completed before Christmas when all the kennels were again full. Down at Cotswold, everything worked as we meant it to and I think even the dogs noticed the difference.

The floodlight highlighted the sparkling snow and everything was perfect!

The design of the new cattery was left to Peter who had looked after the cats since Marjorie left. A concrete base was put down and the exterior walls were built with concrete blocks. We decided the prefabricated galvanised mesh panels we had used for the kennel blocks were not suitable for a cattery so we called in a local carpenter, Bert Tillen, to put Peter's designs into practice.

Following Peter's estimates of the amounts and type of hardwood required, we bought these from a local timber mill. These, together with large sheets of plastic for the pen walls, filled about a quarter of the cattery space. I have a clear picture of Bert, standing in the bare cattery, looking with trepidation at this enormous pile of timber and wondering how long it would take to convert it into twenty cat pens!

Before Bert started work, the usual suspended ceiling was installed. Each pen was 6 feet by 4 feet and had a 3-foot door. When all the framework was finished, it was varnished. The interior fittings provided the cat with a 'box bedroom' with a shelf to jump onto and the roof of the bedroom which served as an observation post/sunbathing area next to the window which was covered in mesh to prevent the cat escaping when the window was opened in summer. The bedrooms and shelves, like the dogs' beds, were painted alternately bright blue and orange.

A section at the end of the cattery was reserved for storage and for serving the meals which now consisted of propriety dried and tinned foods, thus putting an end to the permanent fishy smell. All dish washing was done in the kennel kitchen.

It was pleasantly satisfying to walk down and see a happy cat at each window observing any passers-by. After a couple of years, we found it necessary to increase the cattery accommodation so we lengthened it to thirty pens.

*

It seemed Marjorie had very little control of her finances when she ran the place. Although most of the clients were obviously quite well-to-do scarcely any of them paid when they collected their dog or cat. They just said, 'Send me the bill.' And Marjorie had really no idea who owed her money, or how much! She also allowed customers to board their animals for just one or two days at Christmas and then had to turn away longer bookings.

There were no set kennel opening hours and many of her customers assumed the business offered a twenty-four-hour service. After taking over, we had one customer who arrived at 7 am, before we had even emerged, and was taking his dog past the house to put it in a kennel himself; another called at 11 pm to collect his dog. It was not possible to resolve all these problems immediately because we took over at the beginning of the busy summer holidays, but we dealt with them as soon as we possibly could.

*

Whilst all this work was proceeding in the kennels, we had central heating installed in the house by Brian Green who recommended Maurice Chivers to us as a builder. Maurice came to us just as the rush died down and stayed for well over a year!

His first job was to remove the wooden shed over the kitchen and replace it with a smart office with large windows so that we could see who was arriving outside.

Maurice and Bert at Enborne Kennels

One of the first things we had noticed in the wooden shed, which had been Marjorie's office, was a one litre bottle labelled 'Miss Giddings Diarrhoea Mixture'. We thought 'Poor Miss Giddings!' but it was, of course, a standby remedy for the dogs!

After building our new office, Maurice devoted himself to modifying the other two kennel blocks but he never objected if we diverted him to something else ... like a blocked drain. He was one of the old school who came to work on a bicycle with a shovel tied round his shoulders. We never had a quotation for any particular piece of work, or a bill, but he would come to me about once a month and ask me if he could have another advance. I would pay him what he asked and so we went on the whole time he was working with us.

He occasionally brought a labourer with him - Bert, whose surname I never did know. I should think Maurice must have been nearing seventy years of age and Bert was even older but they were just what we needed for what we were doing. They took quite a real interest in the business – sometimes too much!

A rather genteel lady brought in her very small dog one day when they were working near the office. Bert took one look at the creature and asked, 'What do you feed that on, then? Peanuts?'

Afterwards, we tried to impress on him the need to be more diplomatic with customers!

*

I think the next work we undertook was to make a large gravel car park outside the office bounded by a post and rail fence with a five barred gate opening to a new tarmac drive leading down to the kennels. Before the car park and gate were installed, customers used to drive in from the road, straight down the rough farm track to the kennels, bypassing the office and disturbing all the dogs.

Perhaps I should mention here our solution to the problem of kennel opening hours was soon adapted to match a routine with the dogs: Barbara and I, plus any helpers, went down to the kennels about seven or eight o'clock (depending on the time of year), letting them out in turn and tidying their kennels. Having dealt with the boarders, we opened the gates at 9 a.m. to customers. We closed at 12 noon to feed and exercise the dogs, and opened to customers again from 4 p.m. to 6 p.m. Then another session with the dogs, a 'biscuit at bedtime' and back to the house.

Before dealing with the boarders, Barbara had done whatever was necessary with our own dogs. When she had a litter of puppies, Annette came over to help her, getting up before the other members of her family. From the age of about six or seven, she knew what was needed and wielded a dustpan and brush enthusiastically, cleaning up the puppies' floor. She was a great help to Barbara.

The dogs we accommodated during our thirteen years at the kennels were all pets but, like humans, they varied in colour, size and temperament. Inevitably, one preferred some to others but one tried to treat them all impartially. However, a few incidents are worth recounting.

One of our customers bred a line of prize-winning dachshunds but prize-winners at dog shows win those prizes because of their dog's conformity and shape, not their temperament. I was taking one of this person's dachshunds down to the kennels on a lead when it suddenly jumped up and sank its teeth into the base of my thumbnail. It was quite painful and took months to heal but one had little choice but to grin and bear it.

Another time, a gentleman we had not met before brought in a pair of Neapolitan Mastiffs - large, hefty dogs with wrinkled skins. They both looked very aggressive. The owner helped us to put them in a kennel in Cotswold Block and said he would collect them in two days.

When the time arrived for them to be let out in a large run, they came into the corridor but refused to go into the run and approached us aggressively if we moved towards them. We realised someone was going to get hurt if we kept these dogs much longer so we telephoned the owner who, luckily, was still at home and he came and fetched them. This was the only occasion when we had to admit defeat.

Another tricky situation occurred in what might be termed 'The Case of the Fierce Pyrenean Mountain Dog' or 'The Hound of Enborne Kennels'. The Pyrenean was put in a kennel in Chivers Block which had access at one end through a door to the interior corridor of Chivers. At the other end was a trap door to the exterior corridor and thence through a gate to a large run.

Our tactics for getting him out of his kennel and into the run, whilst preserving our safety, were as follows: Person A would open the gate of the big run and stand by; Person B would call the dog to the gate from the kennel into the interior corridor and keep him there (snarling!) whilst

Person A opened his trap door then quickly escaped through the corridor and door. Person C would stand at the far end of the big run, call the dog down and keep him there whilst Person B closed the run gate. The hound was returned to his kennel using a reverse procedure.

The last episode is a much happier one. One day we admitted a German Shepherd Dog called 'Wolf' for 'a few days'. When we came to examine the dog, we found that he was almost bald around the neck – he had obviously been chained up. We contacted the owner and learned the background. His real owner, who had been the local policeman in a nearby village, had emigrated to Australia under the Government-sponsored scheme and thought they had found a good home for his dog.

But the new owners found that they could not handle Wolf and finally kept him chained up in a shed, looking forward to the day they could pass him on. So we ended up with Wolf on the permanent establishment rather than as a boarder.

Wolf had what you might call a *strong character*; if he wanted something, he was determined to get it. Barbara approved of his pedigree and decided to mate him to Flora, who was in season.

We started the procedure one evening after supper in the kitchen but they did not seem to be progressing very well and we decided to put it off until the morrow. But Wolf had other ideas! When we tried to remove him, we were pinned into the corner of the room – I even had to take refuge in the pantry. So we decided we had no option but to continue and eventually Wolf succeeded and finally consented to go to bed!

Having heard Wolf's recent history, we thought it would be the right thing to do to tell the story to his proper owners and I managed to contact them through Australia House.

Apparently, my letter arrived on Christmas Day and bought great joy to the teenage daughter who had been very attached to Wolf. It then transpired that the family had found that Australia did not suit them; they were coming home soon and would like to have Wolf back. We agreed and a date was fixed for them to pick him up.

Wolf was put in a big run which was clearly visible from one of the bedroom windows and we all went there to watch. His owner walked towards the run and Wolf retreated until he opened the gate and entered at which time Wolf cautiously began to advance and then retreated again. Confidence was being restored!

Eventually, Wolf was in his arms, virtually saying, 'Oh, I have missed you, Dad. Where have you been?'

We almost burst into tears with the emotion of reunion and when they all departed we felt we had been through quite an experience!

*

There were three people associated with the kennels who deserve a special mention: one is Angela. When we first met her, she was about fifteen years old and was tall, strong and silent – she never spoke unless spoken to and even then it was not very audible.

Her headmistress in Newbury kennelled her dog with us and asked one day if she could have a word with us. Apparently, Angela was generally a 'Naughty Girl' in school but she had one saving grace: she was always willing to look after the school pets from stick insects to rabbits ... after school, at weekends and during holidays; nothing was too much trouble. The Headmistress wondered if she could come and work at the kennels for one day a week so that she could find another field in which to exercise her zoological talents.

We agreed and found her a great help. When she left school, she came to work full time and soon became the backbone of the establishment. Her greatest attribute was her determination never to let you down. On several occasions she arrived at the kennels in the morning puffing and blowing and red as a beetroot - a couple of minutes late because her bicycle was out of action and she had to run all the way from Newbury!

If she wanted a favour, which was rare, such as leaving ten minutes early or having an afternoon off, she had one favourite phrase with which she introduced her request: 'Any chance of ... '. We still use it!

Angela had worked for us for several years when one Friday we had an 'Any chance of ... ' for the following afternoon. She returned on Sunday morning and mentioned quite casually that she was now married to a postman called Ron! We met her husband soon afterwards, a very pleasant practical man who obviously adored Angela. She stayed with us until we left but eventually (presumably having saved up some money) she and Ron bought their own kennels near Glastonbury.

We left our own dogs with her several times when we went on holiday and on one occasion, showing the trust we had in her, left a bitch to whelp with her. We like to think that our willingness to give Angela a chance to use and develop her individual talents saved her from being cast out by the system and, instead, changed the course of her life.

Margaret was another character; she was about forty, married and she lived in a council estate about a mile away. Margaret's main interest in life was her horse, Nicky, who lived in a stable in one of the paddocks. In return for free accommodation for Nicky, Margaret worked in the kennels looking after the dogs but she also excelled at redecorating the buildings with our white emulsion.

The other person who remains in our memories is 'Mr Mole', a pensioner who lived in a council house a little way up the road. Every morning we used to hear the 'Click, Click' of his walking stick on the road and we knew he had come to see if there were any more molehills in the grass. He was a wizard at catching moles and he taught me all I know about the art!

*

We had never concerned ourselves with holidays when we were at Cumnor Hill. We owned a small Sprite caravan and we used it to take us and the dogs to various caravan sites in the South of England. Now, after all the excitement of moving and rebuilding the kennels, we thought we needed a break.

Peter, Susan and Margaret were there to look after the reduced number of dogs and cats so we booked a return flight to Zurich with BEA, as it then was, which included a Fly-Drive car. We set off in the evening for Heathrow, working until the last minute and virtually putting our paint brushes down as we got in the car.

We had a civilised check-in at the airport as people were still treated as people in those days, not as cattle. We arrived at Zurich Airport and went to collect the car.

Oh dear! In the last minute rush, we had left our driving licences behind! It was suggested that we contact BEA for help and we spoke to Paddy Murphy who was BEA's 'Man in Zurich'. He said that if we could get the licences to Capt.X, the BEA pilot who would be flying the next flight from Heathrow to Zurich he would take them with him and we could pick them up at the airport.

All went according to plan: we telephoned the kennels and told them what had happened and where the licences were. David Buckwell took Maurice Chivers in his car to Heathrow, Maurice handed them over and we had them an hour later! You would never get such caring service nowadays, would you?

Now the main trouble in taking a holiday from the kennels was that the weather in Europe was always at its best when the kennels were full – obviously. So if we wanted a holiday with good weather we would have to go to the Southern Hemisphere (e.g. South Africa) or to an area where summers lasted much longer than ours (e.g. the western USA). Or we could take a winter skiing holiday in Europe. All of these we did.

Travel by air was easy because Heathrow was only fifty miles down the M4 and Gatwick was not much further. We usually made the journey in taxis. There were very few security checks (unlike today), no 'cheapie' airlines, airline tickets were bought either at a travel agent or by telephone from the airline itself with no fiddling about on a computer.

Hotels were decided either by studying the local tourist office guide or the relevant Michelin Guide and a booking could be made by telephone or letter. Sometimes it was unnecessary to book a hotel – we just arrived, drove around to make our choice, and then hoped they had a room. 'Haben Sie ein Zimmer frei, bitte?'

This might be a good place to express my opinion of the modern holiday. Not only is the population of the world increasing exponentially but of that increase an increasing proportion can afford to take foreign holidays. The result is that all the old holiday resorts are being ruined by overcrowding and new ones are being created in previously quiet villages which either welcome the input of tourist money or resent the destruction of their environment, which accompanies the money.

More and more, the frontiers of the tourist world are being expanded - e.g. in the Antarctic where soon there will be no 'empty spaces' left. It is the growth of the cruising holiday which is responsible for much of this expansion, especially and perhaps obviously, the coastal resorts.

A good personal example of the phenomenon I have discussed is the village of Villefranche-sur-Mer, a few miles east of Nice. We first went there in the autumn of 1973 and I chose the Hotel de la Darse because it was small, in a quiet part of the village overlooking the local yacht club, and reasonably priced. We booked our flight with BEA (or Air France) and picked up a hire car at Nice Airport. The hotel was much as I had expected – about a dozen rooms on two floors overlooking the sea with a balcony for serving breakfast.

It was the proprietress who exceeded my expectations; an elderly headmistress type dressed all in black and sitting at a high desk at the end of the room. The bill she had made out for us had an addition for each day in copperplate handwriting done in pen and ink. I offered payment in travellers cheques in French francs but that was not good enough: she only took cash. 'Je n'accepte que des especes, Monsieur.' A wonderful example of 'La France Ancienne'.

We had several holidays of that type as well as trips to the Western USA.

I referred earlier to the changes which have taken place in holiday resorts. For example, we have visited Villefranche at least half a dozen times during the last thirty years and each time there has been more and more development until, on our last visit in 2005, Villefrance Bay was being used as an anchorage for one large cruise ship every day, each vessel disgorging thousands of tourists into this small village. Horror and ruination!

*

After thirteen years at the kennels I began to feel the chore of maintenance, of having to keep one step ahead of the dogs. At 63, I felt the urge to retire. I think Barbara would have gone on forever but she agreed that it was, perhaps, time to think about retirement.

A few months before this we had been on holiday in South Africa and had looked at housing there. Property and land were much cheaper than England and, while visiting a wine estate, we got talking to a number of English people who had already emigrated. They thoroughly recommended South Africa as a place to live.

The temptation was increased by the fact that since the Sharpeville massacre, when South Africa's attraction to foreign investment had greatly declined, the South African government were offering extremely favourable exchange rates to immigrants. We kept up correspondence with a land agent out there and also checked out boarding kennels and investigated transport from the UK for dogs.

We discovered a steamship line which plied between Avonmouth and Cape Town via Ascension Island and St Helena which would take passengers' dogs in their own kennels on deck. The owner had to provide the food and we soon found we were the owners of dozens of tins of dog food!

Then disaster! One weekend the South African government cancelled the favourable exchange rate and forbade the export from South Africa of more than 5,000 Rands. This obviously killed our plans of moving to Cape Town and we had to look for somewhere to live after leaving the kennels.

We could not both be away from the kennels at the same time so one of us would follow up possible offers from estate agents in the morning and the other in the afternoon. It seemed to be the case that if we found a suitable house the garden was too small and vice versa.

Eventually we found a satisfactory combination in Rood Hill House in Boxford – a five-bedroomed house with half an acre of land and no near neighbours. We paid about £90,000 for the house and received about £150,000 for the kennels. We had to leave the kennels before we could move into Rood Hill House so we rented a cottage close to the kennels and, with the new owners' permission, left our dogs in their kennels.

We all moved into Rood Hill House in the middle of July 1983 with five adult dogs, and two six-week-old litters - sixteen puppies in all.

Chapter 9: Rood Hill House

Rood Hill House in the snow

It is difficult - and would be extremely boring - to list all the things that needed doing to the house. Suffice it to say that they were considerable, and included a complete new central heating system and two prefab kennels with medium sized runs.

We did a lot of the work ourselves; jobs like fitting cupboards and wardrobes in all the bedrooms. The bathroom upstairs was very small – six feet square – so we stripped it and used it as a store room. The adjoining minute loo also adjoined one of the bedrooms so we knocked down the wall, installed a whirlpool bath in place of the loo and converted the bedroom into a large bathroom. Downstairs, quite separate from the rest of the house, was another bedroom with adjoining bathroom which we regarded as a guest room: guests were told that they were too far away to disturb us, whatever they did!

Boxford was an old village about five miles west of Newbury on the River Lambourn. It was a rather mixed village: there were some lovely old thatched cottages around the river bridge, some large Victorian houses and a small council house estate.

Similarly, the population was mixed, varying from older well-to-do folk to commuters to more local workers. The church, St Andrew's, was over seven hundred years old and the vicar was Nigel Sands, a very friendly, capable priest who also happened to be chaplain to Crystal Palace Football Club. Saturday afternoon weddings were strictly limited!

We were both on the Parochial Church Council and Barbara used to play the organ regularly. One of our happiest memories is of the candlelit Carol Service which we organised. It was a lovely evening and the whole church was lit by candles.

We made a number of friends in the village and were very happy there. But Rood Hill House had one drawback: it stood in an isolated position (it was about half a mile from any other residence) and that made it easy prey for a burglar should we go away for a period. So when we went on holiday, Valerie and David Pilley, old friends living in Newbury whom we first met when they bought a puppy from Barbara in 1976, used to move into the house to look after it; indeed they came to regard it as their summer holiday in the country.

We had some excellent holidays while we were in Boxford. The most exciting were our visits to Africa, one of them to the South Luangwa National Park in Zambia where we stayed in three separate camps and where the high spot was a night safari when we observed a leopard who climbed a tree to roost right in front of our eyes.

The other was a canoe safari on the Zambezi River where we saw herds of elephants and hippos in the water. We detoured on the way home to visit Dar es Salaam which was so much more overcrowded than during our time there. We soon fell back into speaking Swahili with the locals and were very well accepted as old friends with 'Habari za siku nyingi?'

We had the use of a car with a chauffeur and made a trip up to Bagamoyo with an African lady guide. She had been educated at an English school and was rather disparaging about the present Swahili school which her daughter attended.

We had a fish and chip lunch, with beer, in a beach café. In the middle of lunch, out of the blue, she said to me, 'Is it true that the last English king was Richard the Third?'

A rapid delving into the history in my mind suggested that the answer must be 'Yes'; after the Plantagenets (Richard III) came the Tudors (Welsh), then the Stuarts (Scottish) and finally the Hanoverians (German).

She followed up this extraordinary question with the statement that her favourite English writer was Barbara Cartland!

We also paid a visit to Oyster Bay where we used to live. Our driver backed the car into a house drive to turn it round and was immediately accosted by several askaris (armed policemen) who questioned the driver and took the camera from my lap. Eventually they let us go and, when I asked our driver why they had acted like that, he said that this was the house of a government minister. They were afraid we might take photographs and send them to South Africa who would then bomb the house!

We found this same rabidly nervous attitude at the airport on our departure. We were both strip-searched three times.

*

Back to Boxford: Barbara bred about forty litters while we were there, some sired by her pride and joy, Yoll, a lovely, affectionate male German Shepherd. The maximum number of dogs we had at any one time was seven.

After twenty-one years at Rood Hill House we found it was becoming more and more difficult (and expensive) to maintain. One autumn, it became almost impossible to dispose of the leaves from the half dozen large chestnut and other trees and any help in the garden was either unobtainable or ridiculously expensive.

House prices were soaring and we found we could sell Rood Hill House for £450,000. We could also buy an adequate property outside the area for a half that price, which is what we did.

I had the idea of returning to our roots in North Lincolnshire and, after one or two exploratory trips, we settled on a bungalow with four bedrooms and a garden of about a third of an acre in Keelby, about eight miles from Grimsby. It was on the market for £200,000.

There was some delay in selling Rood Hill House because the couple who really wanted to buy it were having trouble selling their own house in Windsor. The husband was Andy Swiss, now a top BBC sports commentator, and his wife was a doctor. They were such nice people that we persuaded the seller of the Keelby bungalow to bear with us.

At this time, I was having trouble with my left hip and Barbara had to do most of the packing, including 140 cardboard boxes of books and all the glassware and china, except for one small box which the removal company had to pack themselves under the insurance policy. Naturally,

this had to be the box containing one of our favourite wine glasses ...
which got broken!

Chapter 10: Keelby

We moved up to Keelby on 29 April 2004 with our remaining three dogs in the car. On arrival, we then had to put them into kennels because the garden was not yet fenced. They had to stay there for five weeks!

Soon after they came out, I had my operation in St Hugh's Hospital which entailed a stay of about ten days with light duties only for some weeks after that.

It was while I was in hospital that Barbara took the three dogs - Kiri, Sirius and Amy - into the garden. Amy went into the shrubbery and just fell down dead: terribly sad news that Barbara brought me two days after my operation.

Eventually we settled into a routine with the dogs, the garden and the house. We began by taking Kiri and Sirius in the car to 'Windy Corner' where we could let them run free unless another dog appeared. But we soon realised we could no longer hold them on leads and they had to make do with balls thrown in the garden.

When we first arrived, we thought Keelby Church would be ideal for us because it was so active. But we soon discovered that, by our standards, it was very 'way out', had no time at all for Cranmer's Book of Common Prayer, and enthusiastically took part in the 'Peace' with hand shaking and embracing all round the church.

This was not for us! We found a church in the much smaller village of Stallingborough which was more to our taste, although still with no Cranmer. But we have continued to attend. I took up the post of Treasurer in 2006 when they were desperate and continued for three years until I could no longer tolerate the dictatorial attitude of the priest as chairman of the PCC. I resigned at the end of 2009.

However, we are very fond of the whole congregation and have made particular friends with Mary and John Taylor. Mary has been a nurse for many years and John has been headmaster of a number of schools, finally becoming a member of OFSTED. It is good to be able to discuss old times with them in this part of the world.

I found there were a couple of churches nearby which did regularly use the Communion Service from the Book of Common Prayer - at Brocklesby (seat of the Earl of Yarborough) and at Croxton. At both churches the priest is the Rev. Felicity Couch, a lovely lady who is as much different from the Stallingborough priest as it is possible to be. So we try to attend the Communion Services at Brocklesby and Croxton and the Family Service (DIY) at Stallingborough.

*

The distance from our families prevents lots of parties but we did have two … Barbara's 80th birthday in 2005 and our Diamond Wedding in 2006. We managed to entertain about twenty members of the family on each occasion, probably our swansong – or perhaps not?

In 2006, Stephen, Annette's husband, did not come up on the previous evening with the rest of the family because he was arranging (guess what?) a firework display near Brighton. When this was over, he set off on his motor bicycle and arrived in Keelby at about 4 a.m. He knew he would not be welcome at that hour and settled down in his 'bivvy' to have a sleep in a dry ditch.

He was awakened by the sound of a car stopping and heard a voice reporting in on his mobile radio, "I've found the bike (Guv?)."

Stephen raised his head and said, "Good morning, officer."

He was then asked a number of questions ending up with, "What are you doing in Keelby?"

His unlikely answer was, "I was arranging a firework display near Brighton and now I've come up to my Granny and Grampy's Diamond Wedding anniversary."

The officer suggested he went back to sleep for an hour or two!

On the occasion of our Diamond Wedding, all the family helped to arrange presents and surprises for us.

Susan had a photograph of us on our wedding day and Annette enlarged it and printed it for everyone to sign. Susan then found a clever glass engraver who copied the outlines of the photograph onto a large brandy balloon with the two figures set inside a diamond outline with the names and date added.

Peter found and telephoned the correct number and received the answer: "Buckingham Palace". He gave them the date of our diamond wedding and it was promised that a card of congratulation from Her Majesty would be sent. I was driving down the road that morning when I met the post lady who flagged me down and waved the envelope. She knew what it was. The weather was warm and she was dressed in shorts. I thanked her and suggested that, if she had been wearing a skirt, I would have expected her to curtsey! We had a giggle about that.

*

One person I must mention is 'Tuesday David' – so called because it distinguishes him from all the other Davids we know.

David came to help us with the garden soon after we arrived and he has been with us every Tuesday since. His gardening activities soon extended to other tasks – decorating, repairs, laying slabs, fitting kitchens and bathrooms, etcetera. Not only is he 'Capability Brown' of the area but also 'Versatility David'!

We, and Barbara in particular, have taken great pride in the garden at Keelby. It is about a third of an acre - roughly half of which is grass which is cut once a week in the summer by Steve. There are also several large flower beds and a number of large trees. The long western boundary (200 feet) is marked by a large conifer hedge, on the other side of which is a paddock occupied by 'Dobbin'.

David, Valerie, Harry, Geoff and Brenda at Keelby, 2005

The hedge began to show large brown patches recently – most unsightly - and we had a close-boarded fence erected to screen it. We have had a number of climbers planted along the fence – clematis, rose, jasmine and blackberry - but they are having to compete with the hedge for nutrition. We try to keep colour in the garden throughout the growing season - snowdrops, daffodils and tulips (more planted each year) followed by clematis Montana and a series of perennials through the summer especially varieties of clematis, Barbara's favourite.

One of the reasons we came to this part of the world was that Barbara's brother, Geoffrey Hilton and his wife, Brenda, live at South Ferriby, about fifteen miles to the west. We keep in constant touch and meet now and again at the Thornton Hunt pub - about halfway between us - for a meal.

Keelby is quite a substantial village; it has a post office, a Spar grocery store, a hairdresser, three takeaways, two public houses, a large new sports stadium with playing fields which support several football and cricket teams, and it has a good bus service to Hull and Grimsby, neither of which I would describe as a 'Centre of Excellence' in any way!

It gives me great pleasure to pick out idiosyncrasies in local usage of the English language. The locals almost always greet with a 'Hiya!' and part with a 'Seeya!'. Ask someone (say in a shop) if they can do or provide something, and the inevitable amiable answer is always 'Course I can!' Local nurses always follow a request to do something with '... for me', i.e. 'Can you close your left eye for me?'

*

I had a fall in the garden a few weeks ago and have developed a haematoma on my left leg which needs regular dressing and care. We hope it will not take too long to heal but healing is slower as one gets older.

As I sit here, immobile in my chair, I cast my mind over the close on ninety years since I was born, and the changes that have taken place in my lifetime. To discuss these in detail would, of course, need a much longer book than this but I think that a few closing comments would not be out of place.

I think it would be wise to limit them to my own country and to comment on (a) changes in science and technology and (b) changes in society.

In general I would say that science and technology have improved life for most people by making household tasks easier and leisure time better provided for. But there are two riders to these judgements: does technology provide more equipment and gadgets than people really need? i.e. is the tail wagging the dog? And is some of the 'entertainment' now provided as acceptable and improving as it used to be? Or is it even degrading?

As far as society is concerned, I am sure there has been a noticeable deterioration, largely due to the breakdown of the 'man, wife and children' family as the basis of society. The need, or wish, for women to go out to work instead of staying at home to care for their children and the almost encouraged growth of under age pregnancy have not helped.

These comments are personal and general but are honestly felt. I can only hope, most sincerely, that the breakdown of society may soon be arrested and replaced by an improvement based on the values which have been accepted and cherished for many generations - values that have helped Barbara and me to enjoy a gloriously happy and fulfilled life together.

The end